A CRY FOR JUSTICE

*A Mother's Journey
to Confront the Killer
of Her Children*

Joy Swift

COOL HAND COMMUNICATIONS, INC.
A Publishing Company

COOL HAND COMMUNICATIONS, INC.
1098 N.W. Boca Raton Boulevard, Suite 1
Boca Raton, FL 33432

Printed in the United States of America

Book design by Cheryl Nathan

Unless otherwise indicated, all photographs are courtesy of Joy Swift.

Library of Congress Cataloging-in-Publication Data
Swift, Joy
A cry for justice : a mother's journey to confront the killer of her children / Joy Swift.
    p.   cm.
  ISBN 1-56790-084-4 : $17.95
  1. Juvenile homicide--Missouri--Climax Springs--Case studies.
2. Swift, Joy. 3. Victims of crimes--Missouri--Climax Springs-
-Biography. 4. Dyer, William. 5. Murderers--Missouri--Climax
Springs--Biography.   I. Title.
HV6534. C57S95   1994
364.1'523'092--dc20   93-50604
[B]   CIP

Each year, tens of thousands of us fall victim to violent crime only to be victimized again by the criminal justice system that is supposed to be on our side. This book is dedicated to all the wounded soldiers who continue to seek justice beyond a system that lost sight of justice long ago.

Contents

Chapter 1

Family Plan

I knew it wasn't really Greg, but I watched as the wispy figure dodged and darted, and dared the goose to chase him. The huge Canadian goose honked its indignation and charged at the boy. I almost laughed at the comedy of it all. His older brother Steve stood a few yards away gathering smooth stones along the bank and skipping them across the shimmering surface of the cemetery lake. I counted the skips...one, two, three...six skips before the rock skidded on the water and sank out of sight. Little Tonya pulled a piece of stale bread from her sack and held it out, her sweet three-year-old voice coaxing a mother duck to take it from her. She snatched her fingers away as the duck grabbed for the treat and waddled to safety. Victorious, she pulled another piece of bread from the sack to try again.

Stephanie, too old to play with ducks and geese and skipping rocks, had chosen a spot on the island, and sat with her back against a sun-warmed rock to read a book with a bright red cover. But where was Baby Stacy? She was much too young to be left unattended so near the water. She wasn't with Steph. Nor was she with Steve.

The image shattered. As quickly as it had come it was gone. Granite shards of reality came to rest in a neat little row at my feet, the names of the children etched deep into their red polished faces. The lake before me lay silent, empty and lifeless but for the brisk February breeze that stirred its surface. Even the ducks and geese were gone, flown south for the winter. The trees around me stood naked, the grass brown and dry.

My gaze fell on the five stones. We had buried them by age, Stephanie to Stacy, seventeen years to seventeen months. It was hard to imagine that five months had already passed. I wondered if spring would ever come, so the grass around the graves could finally take hold and make them look more permanent.

It was a fitting place to bury them, if there was such a thing as a fitting place to bury children. Mount Moriah felt as much like a park as a cemetery. Our family had come here often to honor dead loved ones. At least George and I came to honor them. But these were mostly grand- and even great-grandparents to the kids, and they all died before the kids were even born.

So, while the children understood the need for reverence here, they mostly came to have fun. I smiled remembering how they loved to run through the halls of the mausoleum, playing hide and seek, jumping out from behind the marble walls to scare a sibling. Their playful ghost-like sounds echoed against the massive marble walls and then came back to haunt them, sending them scurrying to us.

They played tag out on the lawns, dodging through the trees, chasing squirrels and each other as we made our way down to the old stone bell tower and Granddad's grave. The lake and the island were their favorites, and they rarely forgot to bring bread for the ducks and geese that lived there all summer long. Only Stacy was too young to appreciate the possibilities of this place.

. I bent down to wipe a spot from Steve's marker, and brushed away a clump of grass that threatened to cover the first two letters in his name. It seemed ironic the children were buried under the same soil they once played on, and yet somehow more proper than burying them in some unfamiliar place.

What wasn't fitting was that they were dead. The tears came now, coursing down my cheeks in a silent flood of agony. George and I had worked so hard to get our family together. It had taken years to finally get custody of them all, to get ourselves settled into our own home in the Ozarks and start living the life we always dreamed about. After all the struggles we'd been through to make it all happen, the deaths of the children seemed even more unfair.

I thought about Billy. I wondered what he was thinking as he sat in his jail cell awaiting trial. At least he'd be tried as an adult. But that didn't bring back the kids. Nothing the judge could do to him would bring them back.

More than anything, I just wanted to know why he did it. How could a fourteen-year-old boy even think of committing such a horrible crime? A boy I had trusted, even tried to help. A boy who played with our children and then killed them with no more regard for their lives than for the mice he fed to his pet king snake.

And what of this twenty-year-old Ray, who was willing to help Billy murder my children without even knowing their names. I couldn't put a face on this killer, and couldn't think of anything more senseless. If only there had been some motive—justifiable or not, just a reason in Billy's own mind as to why he murdered them—so I could place the blame on something tangible. Motive or not, I could never forgive him for what he had done.

My mind reeled with unanswered questions, but I knew better than to push George into talking about Billy. We had been able to share every aspect of our grieving except this one. Perhaps it was the ex-policeman in him. Maybe it was just his way of dealing with the grief. George didn't seem to care whether Billy was sorry or not and held no curiosity for Billy's accomplice. But I needed to know. For my own healing, I needed to know how the killers felt about what they'd done.

George pulled me to my feet and held me tight until the tears burned away. We walked arm-in-arm to the pickup and paused before passing through the heavy iron gates that marked the entrance back into the real world.

* * *

It was an odd feeling to be just two people after being seven for so long. Odd, because when you got right down to it, George and I never really were just a couple. George was already a father of three when we started dating, so a family had naturally been a part of our future plans.

The Missouri Ozarks were also part of that plan because that's where our hearts were, and that's where we met and ultimately fell in love. George's weekend cabin sat right next to my uncle's, and I had spent many summer weekends with my cousins just for the opportunity to watch him.

I was only twelve when I fell in love with him although it would take him three years to learn that. It didn't matter that he was twenty years older than I. George was the most handsome man I'd ever met. His brown curly hair and impish little-boy grin drew me to him. He also had a special down-to-earth style. Something about him told me here was a self-made man who danced to the beat of his own drum. I admired him from a distance and secretly dreamed of one day being his.

Sunday evenings, we grudgingly packed the cars to head back to Kansas City where my father, my uncle and George all worked as police officers at different precincts. My dad was to quit the department the following year to go into business for himself. My mother had a full-time office job, which left us four kids home alone to raise ourselves and to grapple for attention whenever Mom and Dad weren't too tired from working.

Over the years George became a sort of counselor for me, an adult I could depend on when I needed someone to talk to or to care when no one else did. It wasn't until the summer of 1972 that he started to look at me as an attractive young lady. The first time he kissed me, I knew I would stay with him for the rest of my life.

George was everything I dreamed he would be. He was tender and caring, mellowed by his extra years. I loved the way his soft hazel eyes sparkled when he smiled at me. We spent hours forming our dreams and future plans. We would raise a family far out in the country, the Ozarks, where no one would care about the difference in our ages.

It was always understood that his three children would be a part of that family, and I relished the thought. Stephanie, Steve and Greg were beautiful children; since they were a part of the man I loved, it was only natural for me to love them, too. We planned to have more children after we married, but only to add to the family he already had.

We would have married immediately if circumstances had allowed. But George's divorce from his first wife was not yet final. He had offered Jean everything in exchange for unlimited visitation rights. But her attorney was out for more.

Three pre-trials would take place over the next year, involving a bitter dispute over a family trust fund that wasn't even George's until his mother died. Her attorney wanted the trust signed over to the children. But Grandfather's terms were specific, and the trust could not be altered.

I don't think either one of us really thought about what it was going to take to allow us to marry, even after the divorce. When I was with George, my age seemed so unimportant that I refused to believe

I was still under my parents' rule. I knew what I wanted, and I wanted nobody to tell me I could not have it.

So we kept our dating secret for months, portraying a wonderful platonic friendship for family and friends. We didn't fool my parents for long. They soon noticed the look in our love-struck eyes. George knew he must do the honorable thing and talk to my father.

To my surprise, Dad gave us his blessing and allowed us to date freely. I proved myself more responsible than I'd ever been to show my parents I was mature enough to handle this relationship. I was doing great ... until I got pregnant.

We didn't tell them. Along the end of the first trimester, Mom became suspicious. It was a ten-dollar wedding: a courthouse ceremony before a judge, with only Mom present to serve as a witness. Dad had just started a new job and didn't want to ask for time off to watch his fifteen-year-old pregnant daughter marry a man twice her age. We invited Mom and Dad over to our new apartment afterwards to share a glass of wine and dine on carry-out tamales and chili.

Soon after that, we became the proud parents of the most beautiful baby girl in the world, Tonya Joy Swift. So tiny and rosy pink with big brown eyes and blonde peach-fuzz hair—I marveled at her perfection. I vowed I would be the best mother possible, and because I missed my own mother while growing up, I promised to always be home and available to my children.

Within six weeks of Tonya's birth, we gained custody of Stephanie. Barely thirteen, Steph was just beginning to taste the gangly rebellious freedom of being a teenager, and Jean didn't quite know how to handle it. Any problems Steph was having would have rolled off of George like water on a duck's back. That was George's way. But I wondered, the day he brought her home, if her adolescent misbehavior would crimp our newly wedded bliss. He wanted so much for us to be a family. He hadn't even told Steph about the baby. I wondered how she'd take the news.

The minute they walked in the door, George picked up the baby and handed her over to Stephanie.

"Steph," he announced. "Meet your new baby sister."

Steph's eyes lit up like a kid on Christmas morning. She took the infant in her arms and cradled her like a puppy. Tonya gurgled and grinned; her gaze locked on the matching brown eyes of her big sister. George and I stood silently in the background, soaking up the moment, watching as two hearts melded together. It was going to work! The two families could become one.

* * *

In the months that followed we all learned to work together. Stephanie and I got along real well as long as I didn't try too hard to be her mother. She let me play the mother role; cook the meals, do the laundry and clean the house. And she especially appreciated help with her homework. But I couldn't make her eat her peas.

Shortly after Steph came to live with us, we moved our family to Clay Center, Kansas, where George landed a job as a welder for a farm implement manufacturer. It wasn't the Ozarks, but it was small town living, and the slower-paced lifestyle suited us.

For a year and a half we waited for Jean to give the two boys permission to come visit, but she would not consent. She allowed George to see them only at her apartment, which was in direct violation of his visitation rights. George, not one to make trouble, accepted her terms in hopes of softening her resolve. Finally, in July of our second year, we received a call from Jean asking if she could put Greg and Steve on a bus to come stay with us for a few weeks while she took a vacation. We were thrilled! The extra bedroom was quickly converted into a room for the boys, with matching patchwork quilts on two camp cots and plastic milk crates to hold baseball mitts and Matchbox cars.

We were late getting to the bus depot, and I worried that nine-year-old Greg and Steve, eleven, would feel abandoned in this strange town. I hardly recognized them when they stepped out of the bus depot dragging suitcases nearly as big as they were. Summer vacation was already two-thirds gone, and their overgrown sun-bleached hair and tanned young bodies left no doubt that they had spent the greater part of the summer poolside. There would be no pool where we lived. I hoped they wouldn't be disappointed. I wanted so much to make their stay memorable.

We had so much catching up to do on the way home that I didn't mind the two-hour drive. We talked about old times as all the memories of those weekends at the lake came flooding back. Steve used to come to my uncle's cabin carrying a little wooden bat and a rubber ball.

"You wanna pway bawl?" he would ask.

I always did because I was secretly in love with his father, and playing with his children brought me closer to him. I used to carry Greg on my shoulders along the beach in search of fingertip-sized frogs. We'd return to the cabin with a jar full and enough driftwood and sand to build a miniature world for them to live in inside a wash-tub. Even then I used to secretly pretend the boys were my own sons.

Now I really was their stepmother, a word I hated, but a position I loved with all my heart. These were my sons as surely as if I'd given them life. I wanted them to stay with us and be a part of our family.

But we were only given two weeks, which flew by far too quickly. George called Jean to ask if we could keep the boys for the rest of the summer. She agreed.

We crammed as much quality time as we could into those weeks. Greg and Steve loved their new little sister. Greg especially liked to pick out Tonya's clothes and help her dress. She came out of her room in the weirdest assortment of stripes and polka-dots, purple and green, but with a very proud big brother beside her. Playing hide-and-seek with a toddler was a blast, and jumping up and down in the crib together brought roars of laughter that shook the rafters of our sixty-year-old home.

As summer slipped through our fingers, we again came to grips with the fact that school would soon start and the boys would have to return to their mother's home. George was desperate. He called Jean again to bargain with her. He was willing to do anything to keep the boys, even if it meant moving back to the city. He'd bring the kids over as often as she wanted. He'd even continue to pay child support, if she'd just agree to let us keep the boys. After some consideration, she agreed to give it a try.

George quit his job the very next day. We packed up our furniture and moved back to Kansas City three days later. There were no regrets. It was worth the sacrifice, we told each other. Someday we would return to a small town when we were certain we could all go together. Soon after settling into our new home, we were thrilled to learn that my recent morning cramps were the result of another Swift-to-be.

* * *

Stephanie spent much of the next school year moving between our house and Jean's. She enjoyed the privacy of her mother's apartment (something greatly lacking in our full house), but found too many times that she and her mother clashed, and she would come back to live with us for a while.

Greg and Steve went through the pregnancy with me, learning where babies come from, how they grow and change, and feeling the baby kick inside my tummy. It was a wonderful lesson for them.

The boys were easier on me than Stephanie was, perhaps because they were younger. They didn't call me "Mom," but I was the mother of the house. I could make them eat their peas. The boys, too, appreciated help with their homework, and I wasn't so far removed from my own school years that I couldn't relate to what they were learning. We felt a certain camaraderie suffering through those tough history assignments together.

In April, Stacy Kathryn, a chubby little ball of fire with blonde peach-fuzz hair and Indian brown eyes, fought her way into the world and joined our ranks. We had a wonderful time getting to know her. Tonya, now two years old, counted her tiny fingers and toes, and marveled that she was so real. Steve was quite twinkly-eyed over this tiny new being. Greg couldn't wait to hold her.

"Can I feed her some baby food?" he asked anxiously.

"No, Greg," I soothed. "Baby Stacy won't be ready for real food for several months."

Those months passed quickly, and Greg delighted in the messy job of spooning cereal and bananas into Baby Stacy's mouth. It didn't take long to learn that Greg and Stacy were soul mates, out for adventure and good loud messy fun. Stacy loved his comical boyish charm. Together they could destroy a room in seconds.

Steve preferred the less messy jobs of rocking her and holding a bottle of juice, but he was the more responsible one. Steve and Tonya were quiet and artistic, enjoying involved games of skill and concentration. While Tonya and Steve became engrossed in creating elaborate castles and towers with blocks, Greg and Stacy stacked them quickly and gleefully knocked them down.

Stephanie came back to live with us again and got to know her new baby sister. But she was now sixteen and too busy with her own life to get involved with infants. The boys, however, were a tremendous help, saving me hours of labor simply by entertaining the little ones while I did the housework.

I was also baby sitting my one-year-old nephew, Little Jack, during the day to earn money for Christmas. It's hard to believe, even myself, that I was a mother of five at the ripe old age of eighteen. But I loved it and wouldn't have traded my life for all the riches in the world.

Chapter 2

The Boy Next Door

Moving day arrived! The U-haul was all packed and ready to roll. Our excitement was at fever pitch. Although it wasn't the best time of year to move to the Ozarks, that's what made it so totally "Swift" in its concept. In the dead of February, with no promise that George would make it as a paint contractor on his own, we had bought a house and were moving our family to the Lake of the Ozarks at last!

Bright and early Saturday morning, our caravan pulled out of the old driveway in Kansas City and headed for the highway out of town. Steve and his Irish setter, Robin, rode with George in the twenty-four-foot U-haul truck, while Greg rode along with me in our pickup to help with Tonya and Stacy en route.

Stephanie had chosen to stay in Kansas City with her mother. But we had grown accustomed to her wanderings and felt confident she would soon come to her senses and join us at the lake.

The trip was filled with anticipation. We drove two hundred miles out of the city to the winding roads of freedom. Even the pickup's flat tire seemed like part of the initiation to our new lives in the Ozarks. A quick patch job at a corner gas station, and we were back on the road with just a few more miles to go.

Just past the tiny village of Greenview, we pulled off the main highway and onto Lake Road EE. We followed the roughly paved road up and around, catching glimpses of the frozen lake through the trees. Tonya bounced on Greg's lap as she peered through the windows, impatient for our house to appear.

The kids hadn't seen the place before, but George and I were sure they would approve. With a grand total of only 720 square feet, not counting the deck off the sliding glass door in the living room, it was going to be a tight fit for a family of our size.

The place was built to be a weekend cabin, but it was all we could afford at $15,000 with easy owner terms. Besides, the lot measured nearly an acre, and we figured we could add on to the house later as needed. Until then, we'd just make do with what was there. This was the Ozarks, the fulfillment of our dreams!

"There she is, kids!" I cheered, honking the horn three times to celebrate our arrival. The unpretentious little cottage stood in a clearing, dark and empty, just waiting for us to move in and make her home.

The kids giggled with glee as we piled out of the vehicles. It took everything Steve had to control Robin on her leash as she sniffed out her new surroundings. George unlocked the front door and the kids pushed their way inside, Steve leaving me with the leashed red bundle of energy. They ran chattering from room to room, opening every closet and cabinet door.

George and I stepped outside to suck in the fresh air and survey our newfound paradise. The exterior of the cabin was painted white with black trim, a bit drab for a lake place, I thought. But George, being a painter now, figured come spring we'd give it some color and liven it up a bit.

It stood on a hill several hundred yards above the water. We couldn't afford to be on the lake, but we had a beautiful view of it in the winter, which, unfortunately, would be blocked by foliage come spring. Woods surrounded us on three sides.

To the left stood a summer Baptist church, opened only during the peak tourist season. And beyond it, a mobile home owned by a widowed lady named Mrs. Larson. From there, several dirt roads funneled down toward the lake where a dozen or more resorts shared the three-mile-long peninsula jutting out into the Little Niangua Arm of the Lake of the Ozarks. None of the neighboring houses could actually be seen from our place, so we felt a seclusion we'd never known before.

I looked out over the trees, imagining the colors that would splash out across the hills in the fall and basked in the victory of being here. Robin pulled at her leash, lunging for a squirrel that scurried up a tree. I pulled her back and knelt to pet her.

Robin had come into our lives when Stacy was only three months old, a wriggling long-legged curly-eared pup hidden inside George's jacket. The pup had taken to Steve right off, and he quickly claimed her for his own. He did a fine job of training her to sit, stay and fetch. Now she was a playful full-grown one-year-old, and she sure seemed to like the sights and smells of her new country surroundings. She had me so tangled up in the leash that I could hardly move. George retrieved a chain from the floor of the U-haul and led Robin to a tree to secure her while we unloaded.

With all of us working together, we had the truck empty by the end of the day. We put the boys in one of the two bedrooms, setting up the bunk beds we built before the move. We organized the girls' things in the other room. Tonya was thrilled to find a bird's nest in the small tree outside her window.

We turned the big living/dining room into three rooms—stealing one corner of it for the master suite and even had enough room, after two couches and the dining table, for my sewing machine and a desk for the boys to do homework. I kept busy hanging curtains and pictures while George hooked up appliances in the kitchen and utility room.

When we finally got it all unpacked, everyone seemed quite content with our tiny abode. The boys said it reminded them of the cabin they'd had years back, with its paneled walls and candy-striped carpeting.

The boys were enrolled in the Camdenton schools; Greg in sixth grade, and Steve in eighth. They didn't seem to mind the thirteen-mile bus ride to school and had no trouble making new friends.

Within a month George was hooked up with a building contractor and had all the painting jobs he needed. Steve, who had just turned fourteen, landed an after-school job at the Flame Resort two miles away and quickly gained the confidence of his employer. He cleaned rental boats, pumped gas, and maintained the lawn and beach areas. They had a couple of horses, too, and he was learning how to take care of them.

Within weeks after we settled in, Stephanie was on the phone wanting to come back and live with us. We made space for her in the girls' bedroom, and our family was complete once again.

George was pretty disappointed to learn that she'd dropped out of school while living with Jean, though he couldn't blame her for not wanting to attend the inner-city high school. Still, we hoped she would come to her senses and go on back to graduate. In the meantime, she took a job as a waitress at a nearby cafe.

We added another dog to the family when Steph came back to live with us: a black-and-white spotted mongrel. She named him Lucky because we'd rescued him from the humane society gas chamber. He was a silly dog, not very bright, but Stephanie loved him. With dogs and children to fill our days, we were more content than we had ever been.

* * *

March and April brought gray skies and mud. Afternoon downpours called "frog stranglers" kept us inside more, but not completely. George taught us to live in harmony with the weather. According to his philosophy, there were two kinds of people: those who get wet, and those who feel the rain. George was a rain feeler and rather enjoyed sitting on a fence in the rain. The rains brought life to every living thing. The budding trees that surrounded our Ozark cottage were proof and promise we'd have a rich green spring.

For Easter, George brought home five tiny bundles of peeping yellow down: one for each child. We kept them in the utility room until they were old enough for a pen outside. Greg and I constructed a class-A duck house out of wood scraps, and we filled a child's wading pool for them to swim in.

Stacy celebrated her first birthday the week before Easter. She was built like a Mack truck, and loved chasing the ducks around the yard with Tonya. Tonya went nowhere without Baby Stacy right at her heels.

Tonya dearly loved having a baby sister to play with, but she watched in envy as the boys boarded the bus each morning. She longed for the day when she too could ride the "cool bus." In her mind, school must have been a wonderful place filled with all kinds of things to do. She loved to get out her little toy school desk and make assignments on the little chalkboard.

In the evenings, while the boys did their homework, she got out her coloring books and sat at the table to do her own. Her tongue licked the sides of her mouth as she colored, concentrating seriously on her work. Each afternoon she watched anxiously for the big yellow bus to appear. She could hear it rumbling down the road and always ran to greet her brothers at the door. Stacy was always right behind her, following Big Sister's every lead.

Steve couldn't stay long, but always took a moment to greet the girls before heading off to work. The bus took a circle at the end of the peninsula and passed our house on its way out, so Steve was able to drop off his books and change clothes, then jump back on the bus for a free ride to work.

Greg usually took the time to play with them for a while, remembering what it was like to be the youngest. But Tonya couldn't wait for summer to come, so the boys would be home all day.

It was late in May that Mrs. Larson's son Ron moved in, bringing with him his fiancee and her fourteen-year-old son, Billy. Mrs. Larson must have thought it nice that two boys just about Billy's age lived right next door. The very day they moved into the trailer, Greg and Steve happily brought him home and introduced us to their new-found friend.

George and I looked up from the last bites of dinner to greet the dark-haired boy. There was nothing about his appearance to make us not like him. He was average height for fourteen, though a little huskier than our own boys. His hair was neatly combed and his clothes were clean.

Still, we were both uneasy about this newcomer. Billy was polite when he was introduced, but it didn't seem genuine. He had the most piercing unworldly set of eyes I'd ever seen. Eyes that defied description. Eyes that could not be ignored.

His choice of pets also left much to be desired. A king snake, a good two feet long with one eye poked out, wrapped itself about its master's neck, lending a kind of demonic aura to the pair. I started to ask him how it lost its eye, but quickly decided I really didn't want to know.

"Billy's gotta catch some worm snakes to feed it," Greg said, stroking the reptile along its scales. "Can we go out and help him?"

George threw me a cautious glance. I'd never even heard of a worm snake before, but I guessed there was no harm in letting them go. Just because I didn't like snakes didn't mean they couldn't. I half-heartedly shrugged my approval.

"Go on out," George waved them away. "But don't be pickin' up anything that'll bite."

The boys dashed out the door while Billy sauntered importantly behind them.

George tossed his fork onto his plate, his appetite for those last few bites gone. "I don't like that kid," he said. "I don't know why, but I don't like him."

"They'll be all right," I replied, trying to be soothing. "Give the boy a chance. He's only a child."

George shook his head as he pulled away from the table. "That is not the kind of boy I want my kids hanging around with."

I took his plate and stacked it on top of mine. "We'll just have to keep an eye on them, that's all. At the first sign of trouble we'll nip it in the bud."

"Okay," George said defiantly. "But they play at our house. They're not to go to Billy's."

Greg found the new kid strangely fascinating and began to hang around with him every chance he got. It turned out that Billy owned more than one snake, though the king snake was his favorite. The two boys spent a great deal of time searching out live things to feed the slithering reptiles. Billy usually carried one along with him on their hunts and seemed to thoroughly enjoy watching his snakes kill and devour their meals. It made Greg's stomach turn, but he wouldn't admit it to his friend.

Over the next few months, Billy came to be very influential in Greg's life and more than once Greg was grounded for something Billy conned him into doing. They were small infractions, the ones we knew about anyway–coming home an hour late or running off with Billy before his chores were done. It seemed every time the boys got together some sort of mischief went on.

I couldn't put the whole blame on Billy. Greg was no angel by any means. He loved adventure and would try anything once. But Greg was a chameleon, constantly changing colors with his surroundings. I wished he had spent more time with his true-blue brother than with this new kid who, if colors could tell, would be crimson.

Steve realized within the first few weeks that Billy wasn't worth his time. He had better things to do. I did too, for that matter. But I refused to give up on Billy.

George tried several times to ban him from the house, but I saw a boy who just needed someone to care. He reminded me of myself at his age, just needing someone to care enough to expect certain things from him. Perhaps to respect and trust him when he really hadn't proven himself worthy of it.

On several occasions Billy came over complaining of minor squabbles with his mom or Mrs. Larson. I always listened and tried to make suggestions, but I knew his own home life wasn't as nice as ours. I couldn't help but believe that the discipline in our house would influence him for the good.

I tried to treat him like he was my own, but the harder I tried to instill some values in the boy, the harder he worked to defy me. He always had a smile for me, always addressed me respectfully. He even managed an innocent glint in those deep unworldly eyes of his. But I always knew that, as soon as he turned his back, the glint would disappear. The glint was for me only, to tempt me to trust him when he hadn't earned it.

* * *

Our home was governed by fairly strict rules of discipline, which gave the family a sense of security and routine. Billy was expected to abide by those rules while in our presence, no matter what rules he went by at home, which were obviously few. One of our most important rules was that the kids were not to have company if George and I weren't home. We reasoned they didn't need to be responsible for their friends while they were being responsible for each other.

We didn't leave them that often. Occasionally, I would run to the grocery store and leave the girls under the care of one of the older three. Steve and Steph both had jobs, so Greg sometimes watched the girls while I went to pick one of them up after work. But because Greg wasn't quite twelve yet, we never left him in charge for very long.

George arrived home early one day to find Billy escaping through the back bedroom window. Billy scurried into the woods with George hot on his heels. George grabbed a hunk of Billy's shirt and half-dragged him back to the house. Greg knew he was in for it when the door flew open.

"Greg, you know the rule!" George scolded, clinging to his prisoner, who by now looked white as a sheet.

He pointed a stern finger at Billy's nose. "And you knew you were breaking that rule when you walked in that front door." He paused to point to the door. "That is how you came in, isn't it, through the front door?"

"Yes, sir, it is," Billy squeaked, flashing the most innocent look he could muster.

"Well, if you're man enough to enter my house through the front door," George roared, "then, at least, be man enough to leave the same way. Do you understand?"

"Yes, sir," Billy answered again.

George released his grip and pushed him toward the open door. "Don't you ever let me catch you climbing out my window again."

Billy nodded at Greg and quietly slipped away.

George slammed the door behind him and whirled in time to see Greg making a quick retreat to his bedroom.

"Greg, you're grounded for a week!" he shouted. "And you won't see Billy for two."

Suddenly, over the next few months, strange things began to happen. Unexplainable things.

The boys went outside one morning to ride on the tire swing hanging in the side yard. They ran into the house fairly shaken.

"Dad, there's a dead rabbit in the tire," Steve said.

George followed them outside and pulled the carcass out of the tire. It was a wild one, nearly full grown. We questioned everyone we knew about the dead rabbit, including Billy, whose eyes never told what he was thinking. Nobody offered a clue.

One thing was certain. The rabbit didn't hop into that tire and die on its own.

Soon after that, two of our Easter ducks disappeared in the night without a sound. No feathers. No prints around the pen. Nothing. A third duck was permanently crippled, his legs bent and swollen. From then on he walked on his knees instead of his feet. Tonya was heartbroken.

If only it would have stopped then, we could have lived with the mystery. But what the future held in store for us was beyond anything we would have ever thought possible. And already it was too late to change it.

Chapter 3

Busy Summer

Summer finally came and the dog days of soaring temperatures and high humidity drove us to seek refuge in the water and the shade. The evenings brought little relief from the heat, and the two-speed box fans in each room only blew a furnace of hot air through the house.

Steph got a new job through the C.E.T.A. program and was working at the police station as an office assistant. She was learning secretarial skills and her whole outlook on life had changed. She was working toward a career and she loved it.

The police chief took her to lunch on occasion and treated her like the young woman she was turning out to be. She no longer acted like an irresponsible teenager, but like an adult with plans for the future and a good start in fulfilling them. We were pretty proud of the young lady she had become.

Steve's after-school job went to full time for the summer. He was saving his money in hopes of buying a new motorcycle, and, at fourteen, he was responsible enough to handle one. He had sent for information on several different models and finally decided on a Yamaha 100.

His money was accumulating so faithfully that George took him to the bank and co-signed a $500 loan, so he could get it right away. We had no doubt he'd make good on the payments, and the Tidgrens down at the Flame assured him that as long as he did as good a job as he was doing, his position was secure.

The nearest Yamaha dealer was in Stover, so George and I left the other four kids at home to take Steve down to get the new bike. The salesman, busy when we arrived, pointed us to a shed in the back where it was supposed to be.

When Steve pulled open the big metal sliding doors, the sunlight bounced off the chrome and reflected right back into the eyes of a star-struck boy. His fingers glided over its smooth handlebars and down across the canary yellow gas tank. He pressed his palm deep into the leather seat and then crouched to examine the finer workings of the machine.

"Well, climb on," George prodded. "Let's see how she fits."

Steve swung his leg over the bike and pulled it upright. He gripped the handlebars with his long slender fingers and pressed the brakes firmly. He studied the gauges, familiarizing himself with each one, when his gaze fell on the odometer.

"Dad, it's not new," he whined, his dreams shattered underneath him. He pointed to the gauge.

I bent my neck to read the numbers. "Steve, it's only got three-tenths of a mile on it."

"But they ordered it just for me," he complained. "It shouldn't have any miles on it."

George patted him on the shoulder. "The dealer has to test drive it to make sure it's running smoothly. That's his job."

Steve still didn't look convinced as we trudged into the shop. He picked out a matching helmet and a couple of cans of oil before signing the papers to finalize the deal. He was almost over the odometer shock when the dealer told us he was just going to run the bike down the road and back before we loaded it into the pickup.

Steve's head hung to the ground as he watched his motorcycle zoom away. When the dealer returned, Steve lost no time in checking the odometer. It now read eight-tenths of a mile, and he hadn't even ridden it yet!

When we finally reached our lake road, George pulled onto one of the dirt side roads and unloaded the new toy. Steve was going to take it the rest of the way home himself. He was grinning from ear to ear.

George showed him how to start it and where the clutch was. Steve already knew everything, but he wasn't a smart aleck about it.

He just assured ol' Dad that he'd studied it all out and was competent to drive the thing.

The engine sputtered to life and Steve zoomed away toward home. George and I gathered up our ropes and jumped into the truck to follow him. I was quite impressed with his driving skills, but admonished George at every turn not to get too close in case Steve should skid and fall off.

Steve arrived home to four cheering siblings, and we all took a turn riding on the back while George drove. George was surprised at how much pep the little bike had.

From then on Steve took himself to work, which freed up some of my time, though I missed picking him up and treating him to ice cream. He was such a responsible, honorable young man. I was so very proud of him.

We painted our house in June, mixing leftover paint from various jobs to come up with a rich brown color. The whole family gathered around as George showed us how to box the paint, pouring it back and forth between five-gallon buckets to ensure an even color throughout. He opened another can and poured in what was left, swirling the new color into the old.

"Let's paint the house like that, Daddy!" Tonya called. "All swirly." She danced around in a whirl.

Everybody got a brush and instructions where to start. Even Stacy helped with her own little watercolor brush. She dabbled and dribbled and made a general mess of herself, but she was having fun doing what everybody else was doing.

Tonya had a one-inch brush and tried so hard to spread the paint out just right. Stephanie went along behind her to touch up here and there, and to compliment Tonya on the great job she was doing.

George did the door and window trim in gold, partly because he thought it would accent the brown, and partly because he had enough of it to go around. George loved to paint windows.

When the job was complete, we all stepped back to survey our handiwork. George rested his paint-spattered arm against my shoulder.

"Now if anybody asks what color the house is," he said, "tell them it's cocoa. But if they're real go-getters like your mother, tell 'em it's hot chocolate!"

* * *

Poor Jim's Restaurant was a quiet country cafe with no less than eight tables, one dusty jukebox and a pinball machine stuffed in the corner. It was a gathering place as much as an eatery, where customers freely served their own coffee or retrieved extra silverware. The food was good and the prices fair.

The owners, Stephen and Mary Pyeatt, were a young couple with two kids of their own. Stephen was a down-to-earth kind of guy with unruly brown curly hair and a big floppy mustache. Mary was short and shy with long blonde hair and freckles across her nose. Stephen did the cooking and Mary did the serving.

We ate there often because Stephen cooked up whole plates full of French fries for the kids, and Mary always managed to find some applesauce for Stacy. Several mornings a week George stopped in for biscuits and gravy on the way to work. It didn't take long before we were good friends.

George joined the American Legion, and I became the youngest member of the ladies' auxiliary at nineteen. We began to play Bingo on Thursday nights. I looked forward to the night out away from the house. George found out Stephen and Mary played Legion Bingo too, and soon the four of us were sitting together on Bingo nights. Mrs. Larson was also an avid Bingo player, but she always sat with a covey of elderly ladies toward the front.

Every week we laid our money down for cards, and watched as others claimed the prizes. Afterward, the four of us would go back to the restaurant to huddle over a pizza and try to figure out how we could win.

We came up with all kinds of formulas for picking cards. We kept a tally of all the numbers called and then picked cards with those numbers the next week. But it never really worked. Other than an occasional twenty-dollar pot, we always left empty-handed. But it was fun.

The Legion rented the community center in Sunrise Beach, but they were putting up a new Legion Hall and hoped to move into it soon. Members were asked to help any way they could, so George volunteered to do the painting for free. He'd get started on it just as soon as he finished the spec house he was working on.

Under an old abandoned dock near the spec house George was painting, lived a nest of water snakes. The contractor was worried they would move into the new dock, so he asked George how to get rid of them.

"No problem," George told him.

He took his .22 pistol with him to work the next day and kept an eye out for ripples in the water as he painted. It was good for a couple of afternoons of sport anyway, and by the end of the week, the snakes had been eliminated.

Having served eight years on the police department, George was comfortable carrying a gun. He owned nine different firearms, though only two were ever used: a Ruger Bearcat .22 pistol for plinking, and a Winchester pump shotgun he took pheasant hunting, though he hadn't gone in over four years.

The kids knew about the guns and were instructed never to touch them. Whenever the boys were curious about them, George would bring one out and show them first how to make sure it was empty before fully examining the weapon.

He never handed them a loaded gun, but it was up to them to make sure. They were never to take anyone's word for it. The kids had always respected the rules, and neither of us worried about having guns in the house.

The house that George was painting had a yard of pure Ozark mud-clay, a sticky, gooey concoction that clings to your shoes like barnacles...until you climb into your truck, where it immediately divides itself into two equal parts: the first part remaining on your footwear while the second part smears all over the floor boards.

The day George decided to hook up the garden hose and wash down the inside floorboards (a good reason not to have carpet in a truck), he took the .22 out from under the seat and carried it into the house so it wouldn't get wet.

We had an upright freezer in the living room, but we could never afford to stock it with food. So we used it as a closet for the boys. Their shirts and pants were folded on the shelves, two for each boy, and the door rack served as a filing cabinet for household bills and insurance papers. Even the photo albums were kept in the racks on the door for safe keeping.

George placed the gun inside its box and filed it on the top shelf of the freezer door, and he promptly forgot all about it.

Greg and Billy set up a tent in Billy's backyard and I warily gave them permission to spend the night in it. George had wanted to end this friendship, but I kept telling him that Billy just needed someone to care. The next morning while George was at work, Mrs. Larson came over to tell me that the boys had threatened her nine-year-old granddaughter and another little friend with a gun.

"I tried to discuss it with Billy's mother," Mrs. Larson said sarcastically. "But she won't listen. She thinks the boy can do no wrong. But I know it was Billy, and not Greg, who's to blame. Would you talk to her?"

I agreed to give it a try. I knew our kids were taught never to play with guns, but I had no idea what kind of gun training Billy had. If Greg and Billy had a real gun in the tent...well, it was a frightening thought.

"It's all nonsense," Billy's mother said flippantly. "The only thing Billy has is a BB gun and he did not have it in the tent last night. I talked to Billy, and he said the girls made the whole story up. The girls shouldn't have been bothering them while they were trying to have a camp-out."

I probed deeper. "Are you sure Billy has no access to a real gun?"

"No!" Mrs. Dyer looked offended. "We don't keep any guns here." She glanced over at Mrs. Larson working in the kitchen.

"Look, I can't talk anymore," she whispered. "Mrs. Larson doesn't like my son. She wants us to move out. Billy may be a little ornery, but he tells me everything. If he says they didn't have a gun, I believe him."

Greg also swore they did not have a gun. The matter was never solved.

A few weeks later, Billy brought over a steel trap, the spring type that opens like a steel jaw to capture small animals. He sat on the front porch setting the trap and making it snap a twig in half.

Steve watched a couple of times, considered it a stupid game, and came in to tell Dad what Greg and Billy were up to. George shot out of his chair and made a beeline to the front door.

"Greg! Get away from that thing before you lose your hand!" he bellowed. "And Billy, take that stupid thing home, and don't ever bring it back. Neither one of you've got a lick of sense!"

He slammed the door and went back to his newspaper. "Where does this kid get these stupid ideas?" He said out loud. I just shook my head and continued with the dishes.

* * *

The days were sometimes long for the kids, and they waited anxiously for the Big Bear to come home from work. George had started the ritual of the Big Bear when the kids were small to get them to go to bed willingly. They'd brush their teeth and then scurry away to hide under the covers in anticipation of the Big Bear's raid.

George would stalk them one by one, grunting and growling, and searching them out. As he drew closer, they could never contain their giggles, until at last he pounced on them ferociously, tickling and jostling until they cried, "Uncle!"

As they grew older, they added new elements to the game, learning to stuff their beds with pillows so they could hide elsewhere, foiling the Big Bear temporarily. Their giggles still gave them away.

Through the years George learned that he was in constant danger of ambush by one or more of the little mugs as they learned to catch him off guard coming home from work or returning from the bathroom during a commercial break. He'd always tried his hardest not to be too tired whenever they were ready to play the game. It was always without warning, and required constant collaboration to catch him unawares. But the Big Bear always won, even when he was outnumbered six to one, because he was the biggest.

This fact underscored two very special qualities of the Big Bear. First, the Big Bear was a giant teddy, one the family could love and trust. The kind of Bear you could cuddle up with and feel all warm inside. A Bear that could help solve problems and hug back when the tears came. A Bear with a deep steady heartbeat to rest your weary head upon. The Big Bear was the family's best friend. The Big Bear was also provider and protector of the pack. Mamma Bear and the cubs could rest easy at night knowing the Big Bear was there to keep them safe.

Still, the family never grew tired of finding new ways to try to get the best of our beloved Big Bear. Many evenings we all ended up on the floor in a mass of tickling, wrestling arms and legs. Our family wasn't afraid to get down on the floor and play together. I think families would benefit more from a nightly wrestling match than all the counseling in the world.

George's playfulness was wonderful for keeping the family happy, but when it came to responsibility he came up a little short. If I asked him to change Stacy's diaper before dinner, he usually snookered Steve into doing it for him. I tried to get the kids to make their own beds every morning. But Greg slept on the top bunk, and he'd just stuff his top sheet under his pillow and smooth out the bedspread. Every night George would help him put the sheet back on before tucking him into bed.

"How am I supposed to teach him to be responsible if you do it for him?" I asked in disgust.

But George just snickered and threw Greg a silly grin. Dad was just the biggest kid with the most authority, and, looking back, I wouldn't have wanted it any other way.

Ours was a close family, in spite of being two families made into one. I don't think we could have done anything to make our family stronger.

We'd had the boys for over two years now, and Stephanie for the better part of four. Steve was so busy with his job and his dog that he never seemed to find time to go see his mother. But suddenly Greg wanted to visit her for a couple of weeks. It didn't occur to me then, but maybe Greg needed a way to get away from Billy for a while.

Greg and Billy had recently had another run-in with Mrs. Larson's granddaughter and her friend. They were accused of calling them filthy names. Another petty problem that had not surfaced until Billy moved into the neighborhood. Although I knew Greg was aware of swear words, the ones Mrs. Larson told me about were ones I'd never heard Greg use.

Ever since, Greg had been kind of quiet. And Billy had become even more secretive. Unbeknownst to us, and maybe even to Greg himself, Greg was being pulled into a deadly trap by Billy.

Billy had an unnatural love of violence and destruction. He thoroughly enjoyed torturing small animals, and Greg had seen him do it to mice and other small animals before letting his king snake devour them.

Perhaps Greg needed to distance himself from something he witnessed. I don't know. But for some reason the boy wanted to go visit his mother now.

Dale, a childhood friend of George's, was bringing his paint sprayer down from Kansas City for the weekend to help George finish up a house. He offered to take Greg back with him on Sunday. I only half-heartedly helped him pack, not really willing for him to go. The house was sure going to be quiet without our rough-and-tumble boy. I assured myself that he'd be back in plenty of time for me to get him ready for school.

While Greg was gone, Billy's mother married Ron Larson, and the three of them moved into a resort cabin two miles down the road. At least now Billy wasn't right next door. Maybe when Greg came back, we could keep the kid away. Even I wanted that now. Billy was getting to be more trouble than he was worth. I just didn't know how to give up on him.

Shortly after Greg left, Stephanie started complaining of stomach cramps and back pains. I shrugged them off as menstrual cramps or growing pains; she was so tall and thin. Whatever they were, she wasn't quite herself. A good hot bath and some aspirin seemed to help a bit. If it got any worse we might have to take her to the doctor. But doctors cost money, and we had precious little to go around.

====

Chapter 4

Don't Say Cancer

As the weeks passed, Stephanie's stomach and back pains only grew worse, and she found it difficult to function at work. Still we hoped she'd get over it on her own. She awoke one Thursday morning in August to find her abdomen hard and swollen. I called the doctor from Mrs. Larson's house and arranged to bring her in.

Greg was still visiting his mother in Kansas City, and since Steve and George were both at work, I had to take Tonya and Stacy with us to the clinic. Stephanie didn't have an appointment, but the receptionist promised they'd fit her in sometime that afternoon.

Three hours expired before Steph was finally called in to be examined. Her stomach was so swollen the doctor suspected she might be pregnant. But Steph wasn't even dating anybody at the time. He did the test anyway, along with several others. Stephanie was in a great deal of pain throughout.

The doctor prescribed an antibiotic and told us to return the next day when he would have the test results back. We were all tired and cranky by the time we got home.

That evening while I prepared dinner, I heard Steve come rumbling home on his motorcycle. I didn't think much about it when he didn't come immediately in. He was so meticulous about his bike that I thought perhaps he was shining it up or checking whatever it is you check on a motorcycle.

Several minutes passed before I heard Steve come in and say, "Dad, would you go get my motorcycle?"

George got up and went outside, and Stephanie jumped up to look out the window. The motorcycle lay on its side in the church yard next door, its front wheel still spinning.

Stephanie's face filled with concern. "Joy," she called. "I think Steve may be hurt." She motioned toward his bedroom.

We found him lying on his bed. His right arm and side were scraped raw, and his elbow had a deep gash in it. He'd hit the driveway too fast and skidded across the gravel. The bike tipped sideways and dragged Steve along with it across the yard and beyond.

I tried to wipe the dirt away from the larger wounds with a washcloth and used a cotton swab and peroxide to clean the deeper cuts. But there was so much dirt and gravel lodged in the wounds, and Steve kept flinching away.

George pushed the mangled bike up to the front porch to inspect the damage. The turn indicators were bent and broken, and there was a dent in the gas tank where the fork had come around. Steve would be mighty disappointed when he saw it.

"Steve, what'd you do?" George called as he came through the doorway. He poked his head into the bedroom.

"I was going too fast," Steve groaned.

"The only way you're gonna get all that dirt out is to take a bath," George said matter-of-factly.

Steve propped himself up on his good elbow. "No, Dad," he begged. "It'll hurt!"

"Naw, it won't. It'll feel good."

George left to fill the tub and returned to help Steve into the bathroom and out of his clothes. Steve let out a yell when he hit the water, but soon settled down for a good long soak. He and Steph went to bed early that night feeling pretty bad.

Steve didn't feel up to going to work the next day, preferring to rest and let himself heal. I asked him if he felt up to watching Tonya and Stacy while I ran Steph back up to the clinic that afternoon. He agreed he could probably handle that.

At two o'clock, the doctor told me there was nothing he could do, that I should get Steph to the hospital right away.

"The tests don't tell us much," he said. "But it appears Stephanie may have a tumor. Whatever it is, she'll probably need surgery."

He promised to call and alert the emergency room that we were coming and drew me a map to get there.

We were getting along without a phone in order to cut down on expenses, and Mrs. Larson was out, so I had no way of telling Steve where I was going. With ten dollars in my pocket and a full tank of gas, we headed straight for the University of Missouri Hospital a hundred miles away.

Driving seventy miles an hour on the highway, I prayed to be stopped and given a police escort. We went the whole hundred miles and never saw even one police car. We ran into road construction just outside of Columbia and were delayed quite a while. Steph was by now in a great deal of pain, and I had to stop twice to make her more comfortable in the back seat.

We arrived at the emergency room just before four o'clock. I was given papers to fill out. A chalkboard on the wall already had Stephanie's name on it. I hurried through the paperwork and returned them to the desk.

A half hour passed. I thought this was the emergency room! The hard upright chairs were too much for Steph. She was nauseated from the pain and desperately needed to lie down. She asked me to help her into the restroom, too weak to stand on her own.

Steph collapsed onto the hard tile floor and leaned over the toilet to try to relieve her nausea, but nothing came up except the antibiotic capsule she'd taken before we left home. Exhausted by the effort, she rested her head against the cool tile and sobbed, unwilling to even try to stand up.

"Steph, we have to go back," I prodded. "They'll be calling you." I wet a paper towel to cool her forehead and finally managed to get her up and back to the waiting room.

"Stephanie Swift?" a nurse finally called. She led us to a cubicle where Steph was gowned and finally allowed to lie down. Over the next few hours one, then two, and then three doctors probed and poked her as I held tightly to her hand. Each test brought more pain that was by now unbearable.

One test required the insertion of a long needle into her abdomen to draw fluid. Stephanie winced and then lurched against the pain.

"Hold her down," the nurse told me.

"No!" Steph pleaded to me through her tears. "Don't let them stick it in any farther!"

I held her hand still tighter and bent down to hug her. Her whole body shook against the pain.

They wheeled her down the hall to a room full of machinery. I followed along, never letting go of her hand. A jelly substance was smeared onto a probe and moved across her belly. A crude picture on a screen revealed a large mass on her right side.

The doctors speculated back and forth, but none of them could determine what it was. So they wheeled her to still another room for X-rays.

I wasn't allowed to go in with her, so I went down the hall to a nurse's station to call Mrs. Larson. I asked her to get a message to Steve to have George call the hospital the minute he got home. I hung up the phone and went to wait in a chair outside the X-ray room. Only then would I allow myself to cry.

This child of mine was in so much pain, and I felt so helpless. I would have gladly taken her place if only it were possible. A nurse came over to comfort me at the same time they wheeled Stephanie out. I immediately wiped my tears and stood to meet her.

"I must not fall apart," I said to myself. "I must remain strong for Stephanie."

We were taken to a regular hospital room where a doctor sat down to explain the results of the tests.

"We suspect it may be a ruptured appendix," he said, then turned his attention to Stephanie. "If that's the case, I'm afraid you're going to feel a whole lot worse before you get better. We'll have to do surgery right away. We have several options for anesthesia. Do you think you can handle being awake for this thing?"

Steph was really getting scared now, and we agreed that, although being awake would make swallowing the stomach tubes easier and reduce the risk of choking, it was best for Stephanie if she were asleep for the surgery.

George called at seven o'clock and gave consent over the phone to start the surgery. They wanted permission to do an exploratory because they really didn't know what they were dealing with, and wouldn't until they opened her up. While the nurses prepared Steph for surgery, I was sent back to admissions to fill out more papers. We had no insurance.

* * *

George left Steve in charge of the girls and headed for the hospital in Columbia, stopping along the way at Balentine's Variety Store to let them know the kids were home alone. Debbie, the Balentines' eighteen-year-old daughter and a friend of Stephanie's, offered to take a meatloaf dinner down to the kids and spend the night if necessary. Steve appreciated the meal, but assured Debbie he could take care of the girls. After seeing to their needs, Debbie left Steve in charge.

George arrived at the hospital just after ten and was directed to Stephanie's room. She still hadn't gone into surgery; the operation before her's had gone overtime. The doctor came in with papers for him to sign and then left us alone with Stephanie. She looked so pale and weak. And scared. I couldn't believe how quickly she'd gone downhill.

"It's gonna be all right, Steph," George assured her. "The doctors are gonna get you better."

After they wheeled Stephanie away, we lay down on the hospital bed together and tried to get some rest. At midnight, a nurse came to tell us they'd be moving Stephanie to another wing. We'd have to go to the waiting room down the hall.

George was exhausted, having painted all day, and the straight-backed chairs in the waiting room didn't provide much comfort during the long wait. He stretched out on the carpeted floor and used my purse as a pillow. I'm a hopeless insomniac and sat restlessly, getting up occasionally to pace the floor.

At three in the morning two doctors came in. One had a clipboard in his hand.

"Mr. and Mrs. Swift?" he questioned.

We nodded in recognition and sat down in front of him.

"I'm afraid we're not dealing with a ruptured appendix at all," the surgeon began. "Stephanie has a tumor, which has swollen her right ovary to the size of a cantaloupe."

I looked at him in astonishment. "But how could she swell up so fast? It happened literally overnight!"

"That's the way a tumor works sometimes," the doctor explained in a controlled, even voice. "We want to do a complete hysterectomy to remove the tumor."

The word hysterectomy hit me hard. My heart cried out to Stephanie, realizing she would never know the joy of having a child. I thought of what my own life would be like without the kids. It was something I couldn't even imagine.

George pulled me to him and held me tight, his mind unable to grasp the situation. "Doctor, she's only seventeen," he sobbed.

The doctor grew more serious. "If we don't cut the tumor out it will spread to other organs. We suspect she has a second tumor against her spine, which is causing her back pain. If we can't reach it, we'll have to use chemotherapy to try to kill it."

My mind reeled. Tumors. Chemotherapy? George put into words the thing I dreaded most.

"You're talking about cancer, aren't you?"

The doctor nodded his head. "We prefer to use the word 'tumor' in front of the patient. But yes, your daughter has ovarian cancer."

"So what are her chances?" George asked, gulping back the tears. "What's the best you can offer her if we do the hysterectomy?"

The surgeon tried to look optimistic. "The next five years will be the most critical. If she survives that, she could go into remission. We're talking, at best...thirty-five years."

Thirty-five! It came crashing down like a brick building around us. Thirty-five was nothing! Was that the best they could offer her? George was already forty-one and he had a whole lot of living left to do. It wasn't fair! It just wasn't fair!

But without the hysterectomy, they could offer her no future at all.

George reached for the clipboard. "So, where do I sign?"

The doctors left with the papers to finish the surgery.

I called my parents and asked if they'd drive down and relieve Steve, who had been watching Tonya and Stacy for fourteen hours now.

"Honey, it's already four a.m.," Mom objected. "You'll probably be home by the time we get there."

"Mom, we can't leave until Steph comes out of surgery and we know she's okay."

Dad took the phone and told me not to worry. They'd leave right away. They got there at six thirty. Steve was glad to see them.

George called Jean to tell her what was happening to Steph. She said she'd wake Greg and be there in a few hours. Her car was in the repair shop, so she'd have to get a girlfriend to drive her.

We settled ourselves back down to wait. George fell asleep in his chair. I was pacing the hall when they wheeled Steph past me at six o'clock. She had tubes in her nose and throat, and she looked deathly pale. I quickly roused George.

We stood awkwardly in the hallway waiting for someone to come tell us how the surgery had gone. Minutes ticked by like hours. Finally the doctor came.

"We got the tumor in her ovary." he said. "But we can't reach the one along her spine without risking paralysis. We found a third one up in here." He rubbed the side of his neck. "We'll start chemothera-py and radiation on both of those as soon as she recovers from the surgery. It's a fast-growing cancer, but one that responds well to chemo."

"When can we see her?" I asked.

"She's still pretty groggy. You might want to wait a little bit." The doctor walked on down the hall and disappeared around a corner.

George collapsed into the padded waiting room chair. I perched on the edge of the chair beside him. "I want to see her," I said.

George shook his head. "I don't. I can't."

"George, why?"

His eyes gleamed with tears. "I don't want to be the one to tell her she'll never have kids. I can't tell her she's got cancer. What if she looks up at me and says, 'Daddy, am I going to die?' I can't handle it, Joy. I can't. And I'm kicking myself for not being strong enough for her."

* * *

Jean arrived at seven and was the first to go in and see her. Stephanie awoke to find her sitting beside the bed. George hoped that Jean would answer Steph's questions, so he wouldn't have to.

It was good to see Greg again. He'd celebrated his twelfth birthday the week before, and I was sure he'd grown since I'd seen him two-and-a-half weeks ago. I looked forward to summer's end when Greg would be back home with us.

When Jean came out to join us she was distant toward me. Even Greg was hesitant to talk to me with his mom around. So I excused myself to take a walk down the hall and give George a chance to fill her in on what happened.

As soon as I was out of sight, Jean started in on George. "What's she doing here, anyway? Why isn't she home with her own kids?"

"Look, Jean," George defended me. "Joy's the one who drove Steph here and held her hand during all the tests. You should be thankful somebody was here for her."

"And where were you?"

"I was at work."

"Well, couldn't she have gone and gotten you?" she challenged.

"She didn't know where I was working, Jean. Joy has just as much right to be here as you and me."

I did my best that day to stand aside and give Jean a chance to do her motherly thing. It was hard, though. For a couple of years now, I had been the mother to these kids, and I considered them mine. Now a crisis had hit, and I was expected to stand aside and let Jean be the mother again.

Later that morning, George took Jean down to the coffee shop to give me a chance to go see Steph alone. He still hadn't mustered the courage to see her himself. Steph was still washed out from the surgery and wasn't up to conversation, but I was, at least, able to convince myself that the worst was over for her, and we could head on home.

Jean planned to spend the night in Steph's room and then take a bus back to Kansas City and return Wednesday in her own car. To save a bus ticket, George suggested we take Greg home with us. Jean agreed as long as George promised to bring him back Wednesday with all his belongings. He hadn't told me yet, but Jean wanted Greg to come back and live with her permanently.

Greg rode home in the truck with George that afternoon, and I followed behind in my car. George took the time alone to ask Greg what he wanted to do.

"Your mom tells me you want to go back and live with her. Is that true?"

Greg slouched down in the seat. "Well...Mom kinda wants me to," he stammered.

"That's not what I asked you, Son. What do you want to do?"

Greg gazed out the window to avoid making eye contact. "Mom's real lonely livin' all by herself. I think she needs me. We've been doin' all kinds of stuff together."

"Now your mom's been on vacation the last couple of weeks," George warned him. "She'll be going back to work in a few days. What are you gonna do then? Are you gonna be able to stay out of trouble when your mom's not home?"

"Yeah," Greg answered unconvincingly.

George pulled him across the seat and hugged him close. "We've got a couple of days to talk about it."

We arrived home to the wonderful smell of roast beef and potatoes. The kids clamored to meet us at the door. Tonya was so thrilled to have Greg home that she pulled him into her bedroom and closed the door, so she could have him all to herself. She had a habit of doing that when she wanted undivided attention.

Steve showed us how my dad had fixed his motorcycle. The gas tank was still dented, and one turn indicator was still askew, but the fork was straightened and the handlebars lined up with the front tire again.

"I rode it to work today," Steve said. "I wasn't going to go. But Rosemary said she could watch Tonya and Stacy for me."

Our faithful soldier never abandoned his post. When I told him to watch the girls he did it! And he'd done it admirably for a full seventeen hours on his own.

We talked over dinner, being careful not to mention the part about dying in front of the kids. Our bellies full, George and I went in to take a nap. Mom and Dad stayed the rest of the day and then left for their cabin for the night. They promised to return in the morning so we could return to the hospital.

We entered Steph's room the next day to find her alert and feeling pretty good. It surprised me. She looked so bad when I saw her last. Jean went down for coffee, still uncomfortable about my presence. After making sure Steph was okay, George ducked out to find Jean, leaving me alone with Steph.

"Joy, I want you to see this," Steph said, pulling up her gown. She showed me an incision ten inches long running down her stomach, around her navel, and down some more. A tube ran out of a small stitched hole in her side to drain away fluid.

"It'll heal, Steph," I said, trying hard to hide my shock at the size of the incision. They must have laid her wide open.

"But it'll leave a horrible scar," Steph cried. "I'll never wear a bikini again."

"Maybe not," I soothed, "but there are plenty of nice one-piece suits out there."

The tears came now, coursing down Steph's cheeks as the heart of her fears came to the surface. "Who is gonna love me if I can't have a baby?" she cried. "Nobody's ever gonna fall in love with me."

"Steph, you're wrong. Love doesn't come from the uterus. It comes from the heart. Any man who doesn't love you just because you can't have a baby isn't worth having."

Steph listened, but didn't look very convinced.

"Steph, there's always adoption. Maybe that's your purpose in life, to adopt an older child and give him a chance, like you did with Lucky. You remember? You could have chosen a puppy. But you knew the puppies would all get homes. You picked Lucky to save him. Maybe that's what God's got in mind for you. It'll all work out."

But I knew it wasn't that easy.

Although it would have been just another human being hurt by Steph's illness, I do wish she'd had a special boyfriend right then to see her through the weeks of pain and uncertainty. Someone who wasn't family, who could assure her she was still a beautiful caring young woman.

I would have gladly had another baby to give her when she was ready. I would have done anything to make her life happy. I would have given anything to take her place.

Chapter 5

The Last Weekend

George tossed in bed beside me. I knew what was bothering him. He'd been wrestling with it all day, whether he should let Greg go back to live with Jean.

It wasn't that he was trying to keep him from Jean. He just couldn't see carefree Greg in an apartment, especially all by himself. If Steph or Steve were there it would be different, but Greg was a follower, and George saw no good in leaving him unattended after school or under the influence of someone unknown.

George blamed himself for this mess. Maybe if he'd been more careful to make sure Jean got regular visits with the kids this wouldn't have happened. Days just kept turning into weeks, and with Steph and Steve having jobs, the time was just never right to take them to see her. But Greg hadn't been too busy. He should have taken him.

As much as I loved Greg, I tried to keep my feelings to myself and suffer with them alone. This decision was between George and Jean, his rightful parents. Right now I was an outsider, and I had to accept the fact that I had no legal rights to him.

If Greg went back to Jean, I couldn't get visitation rights to see him. I feared I'd lose touch with him altogether, and it hurt to think about it. How would I explain to Tonya and Stacy that Greg wouldn't be home anymore to play with them?

Greg was really quiet about it. I don't think he knew what to do either. He was counting on that decision being made for him, so he wouldn't be the one doing the rejecting.

On Wednesday morning George rose early to get ready to go to the hospital. I asked him if he'd made his decision.

"I'm not taking him," he announced firmly, trying to convince himself that he was making a responsible decision free of selfish emotions. "I feel it is in Greg's best interest that he stay with us. He's got a brother and sisters to keep him company, and you're here after school when he gets home. That's the best environment for him."

I wouldn't argue with him because I wanted Greg to stay. "So what are you going to tell Jean?"

"I don't know. But I'm going by myself so I can't change my mind. Jean isn't going to be happy."

He was right. Jean didn't take the news very well, but she did nothing to get Greg back.

School started nine days later, and the daily routine of alarm clocks and school buses invaded our lives anew. It was almost welcome because it added a semblance of order to our days. Greg was hesitant about starting junior high, but Steve assured him it was a piece of cake.

George went to see Steph every other day, and received quite a bit of flack from relatives for taking so much time off from work. But he never regretted one hour he spent with her instead of painting.

Being confined in that sterile room a hundred miles away from family and friends was hard for Stephanie. No matter how often he came, she begged him to come more and stay longer. He found himself getting home later and later.

Several times he sent us each a postcard from the hospital gift shop with a special message on the back, just to let us know we were on his mind. The kids were thrilled to get mail, but they missed having Dad at home.

George wouldn't take the boys to the hospital for fear Jean would try to lure one of them into going home with her. A couple of times Debbie Balentine came over to watch Tonya and Stacy so I could go with him while the boys were in school. Then one time George took Debbie with him to visit Steph. It was hard for Debbie to see her friend in such bad shape, though, and Debbie cried all the way home.

Now that Greg was back, Billy Dyer started hanging around the house again. Greg and Steve never saw him in school since they were in the seventh and ninth grades, and he was in eighth. I never knew how he got to our house. It seemed unlikely that he walked the two miles every day. Sometimes he'd get off the bus with Greg and just stay the whole afternoon. But I never knew how he got back home, and he never seemed worried about being late for supper. There was evidently little discipline at home.

Stephanie's condition was fairly stable. She was neither looking any worse nor any better. Televisions were wheeled into the hospital rooms on a rental basis, and a couple of times the rent had expired before we could afford to pay another week's worth. Stephanie called Mrs. Larson to tell us the rent had expired again, and she didn't have anything to do.

George and I arrived that afternoon and paid the rental fee before going in to see her. We were startled to find her body tattooed with big black circles and X's.

"It's magic marker," Steph said. "It tells them where to concentrate the most radiation. They started today."

So that's why she needed us to come. I'd read horror stories about the treatments. Excruciating pain and hair loss. Stephanie was so proud of her long silky blonde hair. I dreaded what the next weeks might bring.

"Are you okay?" I asked, knowing George didn't like to talk about medical stuff. He always tried to keep the conversation light, and off of tumors. But Steph knew she could talk to me.

"It hurts real bad when they're doing it," she said trembling. "But Harry T. Hound kept me company."

Harry T. Hound was a stuffed brown and white dog Stephanie bought at the hospital gift shop.

"They let you take Harry with you?" George asked.

"Yeah. They say it makes it easier if I just focus on Harry and try not to think about the pain."

It hurt that she had to depend on a stuffed dog for courage. Why couldn't I be here to hold her hand during the treatments? If only the hospital weren't so far away.

"Hey," George changed the subject. "The doctor said if you're feeling this good on Friday, he'll let you come home for the weekend."

Steph's face lit up. "Really? Oh Dad, if he does, can you come to get me real early on Friday?" She bounced up and down on the bed. "I want to make it as long a weekend as I can."

George left right after breakfast Friday to get her. I spent the day rearranging furniture to allow Steph her own room while she was home. Stacy would be so excited to see her, and we couldn't have her jumping all over Steph. She still tired easily and preferred the lights dim.

By late afternoon her room was ready with a radio, a small TV, a reading lamp and some Seventeen magazines. I had to move Tonya and the boys into the living room, and George and I and Stacy into the other bedroom to make the switch, but everybody was willing to make the sacrifice to have Steph home.

It was just about dinnertime when Mrs. Larson came over with a message that George was on the phone. I left Greg in charge and walked next door.

"Steph won't be coming home," George said.

The news crushed me. Sunday was our fourth wedding anniversary, and I had so wanted all the kids to be here to celebrate with us.

"She's been in a lot of pain all day," he said, his voice ragged. "They've given her everything they can, but it won't go away. The doctor won't sign her release unless she gets to feeling better."

"Oh, George, the kids will be so disappointed," I cried.

"You should see Steph. She's tried so hard today to feel better. She really wanted to come home."

I trudged home to fix dinner for the kids. All the hours I spent moving furniture had been wasted. I ate little; my mind was a hundred miles away with Steph. Greg and Steve felt my mood and entertained the girls while I cleared the table and grudgingly started the dishes.

The front door opened.

"Joy?" a familiar voice called.

I whirled to find Stephanie hunched over in the doorway.

"Oh, Steph!" I ran to her, but before I reached her I knew the hug I intended would have knocked her down. I gingerly helped her to her room while George retrieved her suitcase from the car.

"How'd you get away?" I asked him, taking the suitcase to put away Steph's things.

"Steph said she felt better so the doctor okayed her release. We got out of there as fast as we could before he changed his mind. She was hurting pretty bad coming home, though."

I pulled a plastic bag full of pill bottles out of the suitcase and lined them up on the dresser. Tonya tiptoed in and sat gently on the bed next to Stephanie. She'd been told we'd have to be gentle because Steph was sick. The boys brought Stacy in and held her back so she wouldn't crawl all over Steph. That huge incision still hadn't healed.

We made a chart to keep track of the pills she should take: The red ones every four hours around the clock. The green ones twice a day. The big ones as needed for pain, but not less than four hours apart. The white ones morning, noon and night.

Steph took them faithfully. But the pain pills never lasted long enough. That last hour would be horrible. I stayed up with her most of the night to rub her back where it hurt the most. The spot was marked with a big black circle. She couldn't take a shower for fear of erasing the marks. If that happened, she'd have to endure a whole slew of painful testing to mark the spots again.

Steph was in high spirits Saturday morning and asked if I would take her to a discount store, so she could get some things. She bought a basketful of little travel-size bottles of lotions, shampoos and creme rinses to take back with her. She found a good fluffy pillow (she hated the hospital one) and a bright cheerful robe that did not have a split down the back.

I picked out a pair of blue jeans for George, and Steph bought a shirt to go with it for an anniversary present. We were in town far too long, and Steph arrived home in agony.

Saturday night she cried all night. I stayed with her all night long, applying a warm washcloth to the spot on her back. George buried his head under the pillow to muffle her cries. Her pain was tearing his heart out. When the pain grew too bad, I ignored the less-than-four-hour warning and gave her another pill.

* * *

Sunday, September 11, dawned bright and sunny. George slipped out after breakfast and returned with a beautiful burgundy vase filled with white daisies, baby's breath and four red roses.

"Oh, George!" I exclaimed. "They're beautiful." I pressed my nose to the petals and inhaled their sweet fragrance.

"Now look," George said jokingly. "There's only two ways you're ever going to get a full dozen of these." He pointed to the roses.

"How's that?" I challenged.

He grinned at me slyly. "You either have to stay with me for twelve years or have twelve kids."

I grabbed him around the waist and pinched him. "I'll opt for the years," I quipped.

Steph's pain had subsided enough for her to join us while George and I opened anniversary presents. She even made it through the angel food cake, but by early afternoon she was in too much pain for us to handle. George drove up to Balentine's Store and called the hospital.

"Bring her back immediately," the nurse said. "We can give her an injection far stronger than the pain pills."

George fixed up a bed in the back seat while Steph packed her suitcase. She didn't know whether to dawdle or hurry. She wanted to stay home as long as she could; she hated being in the hospital. But she needed the injection to kill the pain.

Debbie Balentine offered to come over and watch the kids so I could go with them. Steph put on her favorite dress to wear back to the hospital, knowing it would be days before she got the chance to wear street clothes again. Her vision clouded by tears, she said good-bye to her brothers and sisters. She would never see them again.

As soon as Steph got back in her room, two nurses came in to help her settle in and give her the injection that would, at least for a little while, make the pain more bearable. Steph showed them all the cute little bottles of lotions she had purchased, and they shared her delight. I was thankful for these young nurses who had taken Stephanie into their hearts over the past few weeks.

Stephanie pulled Harry T. Hound from the cabinet beside her hospital bed and set him up next to her pillow beside another stuffed animal, a little woolly lamb she had just recently purchased to keep her company in the hospital.

She hadn't thought of a suitable name for the lamb yet, and had asked the nurses to help her pick a name that fit. But none of the names they chose were quite right either. So the nurses covered a box with white paper and labeled it, "Name Stephanie's Lamb."

All the doctors and nurses were told to write a name on a slip of paper and put it in the slot in the top of the box. Stephanie would then open it and choose a name. Steph was getting a lot of attention with people popping into her room to meet the lamb.

George and I stayed the rest of the evening until Steph was sleeping soundly. We knew the injection they'd given her wouldn't last long enough to assure her a full night's rest and within a few hours, she'd be crying for another. The doctors refused to give her morphine for fear of addiction. But as the pain grew worse each day, I wondered why they didn't just give in and give it to her.

* * *

Billy got off the bus with Greg the following Tuesday, September 13. Steve dropped off his books and jumped back on the bus to go to work. The fork on the motorcycle had slipped around, and with everything happening at once, George hadn't found time to work on it.

Greg and Billy played outside most of the time. I noticed Billy was acting rather strangely, though I couldn't put my finger on any one thing. He just acted differently. I had to run to the store before dinner, but I didn't want to leave Greg and Billy alone. I waited long enough for George to come home before I left, and I asked him to keep an eye on the kids while I was away. I went to the store and picked up Steve on the way home.

Billy was still there when I got back. The boys came in from the yard a short time later. While Greg was in the bathroom, Billy pulled a gun catalog out from under his shirt and thumbed through it.

"Hey, Mr. Swift," he said, pointing to a picture of a tear gas gun, "have you ever seen one of these?"

George glanced nonchalantly at the picture. "No, Billy. I don't believe I have." Greg came out of the bathroom and the two disappeared outside again.

I called the kids in for dinner a half hour later. I invited Billy to join us, knowing full well he hadn't been home since before school. But he declined. He sat on the front porch and waited for Greg to finish.

During dinner, I kept getting up from the table to look out at him. He just sat out there in deep concentration. I couldn't decide why I was so uneasy. What in the world was he thinking about?

"I don't know what it is," I said as I sat back down. "But Billy's acting weird."

Greg finished his dinner and went outside to join his friend. He came in a few minutes later.

"Hey, Dad, can us boys go to the movies tonight?"

Steve perked up at the idea. George and I talked it over. We couldn't see any reason why not. Steph's illness had been hard on us all. A night out would do the boys good. I agreed to drive them if George would pick them up. I didn't like to drive in the dark.

Along the way, Billy started talking about guns. I acted as uninterested as possible to show Greg that it was no big deal, but Greg listened intently.

As we passed a variety store, Billy pointed out the window.

"Hey, do you think they sell ammunition in there?"

"I really don't know," I said dryly. "I've never bought any ammunition. Why do you ask?"

"Oh, I got a cousin comin' into town and we might do some target practice while he's here," Billy boasted.

"Not around my house," I said.

Billy leaned over the front seat. "My stepfather says if I show I can handle one, he's gonna get me a gun for my fifteenth birthday."

His birthday was in October, only a month away.

We arrived at the theater, and all three boys piled out. As I started to pull away Greg came running to ask if I had any extra money "for popcorn or somethin'." I opened the glove box, and out popped a Kennedy half dollar. He looked down at the shiny coin.

"Take it," I said with a smile, "and have a good time."

Greg grabbed the coin with a grin and dashed inside. I looked at the theater sign as I drove away. NOW SHOWING: ORCA, THE KILLER WHALE. Wonderful!

* * *

Wednesday afternoon, George had just about finished the paint job on the new American Legion building. The temperature outside had dropped today and the air was heavy with moisture, so he decided to take the rest of the day off to go see Steph. He'd finish the trim tomorrow and head for another job.

When he stopped by home to change clothes, I asked if I could take the kids out to Poor Jim's Restaurant for dinner since he wouldn't be home till late. He slipped me a ten-dollar bill and kissed me good-bye.

It was cold and foggy by the time the boys got off the bus, and we had to break out the winter coats for the first time. At Poor Jim's we ordered hamburgers, a giant order of fries and milk shakes all around. And applesauce for Stacy.

Mary took the order, gave it to Stephen, and then returned to the table to visit. Greg and Steve excused themselves to play the pinball machine, and Mary complimented me on how well-behaved the kids were, and how polite the boys were when they ordered. She pinched Stacy's chubby little cheeks, and Stacy squealed at the attention. I was so proud of them all.

There was an American Legion Auxiliary meeting tonight at seven, and I had really wanted to be there. Mary asked why I couldn't just leave Steve in charge of the kids and go.

"I don't know," I told her. "George is a hundred miles away with Steph and he left me in charge. If something happened while I was gone I'd never forgive myself."

"What could happen?" Mary reasoned. "Those boys are more responsible than any I've ever met. I wouldn't even hesitate to leave my two with them."

"I know," I said. "But I just have this weird feeling that something will happen tonight. I just can't shake it."

Mary shrugged. "I guess you're going to miss the meeting then."

"I guess so."

We paid for our meals and returned home.

Within minutes of our arrival, a knock came at the door. I opened it to find Billy standing in the darkness.

"Billy?" I said, startled that even he would be out so late on a cold night like this. "Come on in."

Billy stepped in nervously and surveyed the room, seeming to take an inventory of who was present. He looked at Steve, then at Tonya, then at Stacy, then at me, then at Greg.

"Has anybody seen my dog?" he stammered.

"No, Billy," I said. "Greg, have you seen his dog?"

Greg shook his head. "No, I haven't."

Again Billy surveyed the room, pausing clumsily to say something. "Well, my dog ran away," he stuttered. "And the dog my dog ran away with came home. But my dog didn't."

"I'm sorry, Billy," I said. "But we haven't seen him."

Billy looked helplessly about the room. He motioned to Greg, and the two slipped into the bedroom and shut the door. Five minutes later, Billy stepped out and headed for the front door in a hurry.

"I'll be right back," he said. "I gotta make a phone call."

He disappeared into the darkness and never returned.

I felt uneasy the rest of the evening although I tried hard not to show it for the kids' sake. The dogs had been barking outside since Billy left, something they rarely did, as if someone was out there just beyond the trees. The wind howled and shook the window panes. I was glad I'd decided not to go to the auxiliary meeting.

George pulled into the driveway just after midnight. I saw his headlights and met him at the door.

"Boy, am I glad you're home," I whispered, so as not to wake Tonya or the boys sleeping a few feet away.

"Hmmm, me too," George sighed deeply. "It's been a long day." He followed me into the bedroom and started to undress. He told me about Steph, and I told him how spooky the house felt tonight.

"Nonsense," he said, sliding under the covers beside me. "It's all in your head. There's not a thing out there but the wind." He pulled me to him and kissed me.

"Maybe," I said, unconvinced. "But it sure felt creepy here tonight. I'm sure glad you're home."

The dogs quieted down, and only the wind in the trees and the shifting of children's bodies invaded the silence. I bunched myself up against George for security and drifted off to sleep.

Chapter 6

The Last Day

Thursday, September 15, 1977, the thermometer dropped in the night, and the boys broke out their down coats to wear to school. After the boys left, George showered and put on his paint clothes to go finish the new Legion building. With hugs and kisses, he was out the door.

The girls and I set to the task of cleaning and catching up on laundry. Our day progressed at a normal, unexciting pace until after lunch, when the mailman delivered a huge box from Grandma Swift. The girls and I tore into it like it was Christmas.

The box contained second-hand clothes from the cousins for Steve, Greg, Steph and me. There was a globe we'd been wanting for the boys, and two bicentennial bell penny banks for Tonya and Stacy. But the most special item was a framed five-by-seven photograph of the whole family.

It was taken at a family reunion back when Stacy was only two months old. George's aunt had insisted we pose for a family portrait before she would let us go home. I had forgotten about it until now, and as I admired the smiling faces of my children, I couldn't help but admit we were a fine-looking family.

"George will be so proud of this," I said to myself.

I propped the picture up on the television set where he would see it when he got home. Then I started trying on clothes and separating them into piles to put away. Tonya and Stacy ran around ringing their little liberty bells and trying on clothes much too large for them. They were making my job twice as hard, but they were having a wonderful time.

A few miles away, George was in a hurry to finish painting. There was a bass tournament down at the marina, and he planned to go watch the fun. More than anything, he wanted to compete in one someday.

He had finished the window trim and was cleaning out his brushes when Bob, the vice-president of the Legion, sneaked up behind him.

"Lookin' good, George," he said admiring the barn red paint and white trim.

"Thanks," George said. "It turned out real nice, I think."

Bob scratched his head. "Say, George, I know you offered to do this job for nothing. But the Legion officers voted last night to pay you a hundred dollars. I know it's not near what the job is worth, but...well, maybe it'll help with Stephanie sick and all."

He pulled a check from his breast pocket and handed it to George.

"Thank you, Bob," George said, taking the check and folding it into his back pocket. "You tell the officers that, yes, it will come in handy."

Bob was a sincere, quiet man. George and I often wondered how he felt about being second in command under his wife. Doris was a commanding woman who wouldn't settle for being president of the ladies' auxiliary. That would be too much like directing a quilting bee for her, and luncheons just weren't her style. She could be as tough as any drill sergeant, but in a likable sort of way. If any of the men were embarrassed to have a woman president they didn't show it. No matter what needed to be done, you could count on Doris to see it through.

After Bob left, George packed his ladder and painting supplies into the back of the pickup and headed over to the marina. The tournament had already begun.

Shiny metallic bass boats polka-dotted the lake, each with a two-man team. George stood in the drizzling rain, the only man amongst a sea of spectators, judges and fishermen without any rain gear.

When the air horn blew, the boats drifted one by one into shore to have their catches weighed and tabulated by the judges. Over at the boat ramp the line was growing long, as each boat owner waited for his trailer to be backed down the ramp. George went over to see if he could help speed things up.

He got on one side of the incoming boats and another man got on the other. Together they lined up the boats and pulled them up onto their trailers. George was ankle deep in water, and his prized fourteen-year-old kangaroo-hide boots were sopped clear through.

The judges announced the winner amidst an outpouring of free beer and much hoopla and cheering. George was happy for the guy, but he wished that someday he'd stand in his place. It was after five. Time to head home.

With my little "helpers," it took all afternoon to get everything organized, but I was in such a good mood that I just didn't care. I picked out a pair of blue knit slacks and a lavender blouse and put them on "just to be wearing something new."

When Greg got home I showed him his pile of clothes and had him try on a few of the jeans. Steve would have to wait until after work. George pulled in, and I was so excited about the package that I ran out to meet him.

"UPS delivered a big box from your mom, today," I said before he could get out of the truck. "Come on, I've got something to show you." I grabbed his arm to hurry him along.

The minute we walked in the door I should have known there'd be an ambush. But George was ready. Tonya grabbed him around the waist and Stacy around the knees. He fell onto Tonya's bed beside the front door and pulled the girls up to him.

"The Big Bear's gonna get you!" he teased. He tickled and wrestled with them. Tonya and Stacy screamed with delight.

"Big Bear can't get me," Greg challenged from his hiding place in the bedroom.

George sat up straight. "Uh-oh," he winked at the girls. "Looks like the Big Bear has another mug to get."

He put on a show for the girls as he stalked Greg. He lunged into the bedroom with a mighty Big Bear growl. Greg threw himself onto his back and the two collapsed against the master bed, a mass of wriggling wrestling flesh.

"Uncle!" Greg called, admitting defeat.

"All right!" George flexed his muscles in triumph. "The Big Bear wins again." He retreated to the living room.

"What's this?" he called, taking the framed photograph from the top of the television.

I whisked to his side. "That's what I wanted to show you. It's the picture Aunt Georgie took at the family reunion last year. Isn't it beautiful?"

"Why did I ever shave my beard?" he said in disgust, looking down at the clean-shaven face in the photograph.

"I don't know," I said. "You look a lot better with it." I grabbed his full beard and pulled him close for a kiss. "But isn't it a terrific picture? It's the only one we have of the whole family together."

"Yeah, it's real nice," he said. He returned the picture to its place on the TV, flipped on the news channel, and sat on the couch to unlace his waterlogged boots.

"Greg!" He bellowed. "Where're you at?"

Greg dashed into the room. "Yeah, Dad?"

He held his boots up to Greg. Muddy lake water dripped from every hole.

"Greg, I want you to take the laces out, and then run my boots over to the dump."

I perked my ears. "What? You're going to throw away your boots? Your genuine kangaroo-hide boots?" I mocked him.

"Yep," he answered matter-of-factly. "They've given me fourteen years of faithful service. But today was just too much for 'em. It's time to give them a decent burial."

I stared in disbelief. "But in the dump? I thought they'd have to hang over the mantel or something stupid like that."

"Naw, I was only kidding when I told you that. But I'll bet I never find another pair like 'em."

Greg plopped himself down on the floor to take out the laces. Tossing the laces onto the couch, he headed out the door with the boots. The dump was just across the road. Knowing Greg, he probably gave them each a mighty heave, hurtling George's prized boots into the half-filled pit.

An hour later I drove to the store to get something for dinner. I got to talking to the check-out girl, who asked if we planned to play Bingo that night. I hadn't even thought about it being Thursday night. We hadn't gone out since Steph went to the hospital. With that hundred-dollar check, maybe we could afford to go after all.

When I went to pick up Steve at work, I noticed a little yellow bicycle with training wheels in the yard. Tonya's fourth birthday was only twelve days away, and more than anything she wanted a bicycle like her brothers.

"Do you think they'll sell it, Steve?" I asked.

"They might," Steve said. "Their daughter just got a new one for her birthday."

I went into the office to talk to Mr. Tidgren about the bike while Steve added up his hours to get his paycheck.

Mr. Tidgren leaned back in his chair to think. "I'll talk to my wife about it and let you know."

We had tamales and chili for dinner. Stacy sat in her high chair and smeared beans all over her front. She always made a mess of herself on chili nights. Steve reminded us that tomorrow was picture day at school, and I admonished the boys to please at least pick out a nice shirt to wear.

"I'm just gonna wear this one," Steve said pointing to his favorite green T-shirt he had on.

I hinted that he might find something nicer in his pile of new clothes. I waited until after dinner to remind George that it was Bingo night if he wanted to go.

"I'll think about it," he said.

I cleared the table quickly, just in case he agreed to go. Seeing my enthusiasm, he called the boys to him.

"You wouldn't mind if Joy and I went out tonight, would you?"

"Aaah, Dad," Steve whined. "You guys always get to go out."

"Now, Steve," he reprimanded him. "Joy and I haven't been out since Steph got sick. We let you boys go to the movies Tuesday. Don't you think it's our turn?"

"I guess," Steve said.

George chucked him under the chin. "You don't really mind, do you, Steve?"

"Naw, I guess not. It'll be okay."

George pulled him into his lap and tickled him. Greg joined in to help, and Tonya crawled up to assist them even more. Though outnumbered three to one, George won. George always won.

I pulled Stacy out of the high chair and sprinted into the bathroom carrying the chili-smeared child at arms length. I plopped her into the sink to wash her down.

George changed into a pair of overalls and dug out an old green knit shirt he hadn't worn in ages.

"I'm gonna head on out to the car, honey," he called as I raced to the utility room to toss Stacy's hand-washed plastic pants into the dryer.

"Okay," I called back. "I'll be out in a minute." I checked my watch. It was after seven.

I kissed the children and told them to be good. Tonya looked at me with her big brown eyes.

"Can I go with you, Mommy?"

"Not this time," I soothed. "We'll all do something together this weekend, I promise." I stepped out the door.

It was quite a bit colder than I expected. I ran back in to get a sweater. Stacy wrestled me for the door as I tried to leave.

"Go baa-baa," she said.

I called for Greg and asked him to fix her a bottle of juice. He jumped right up and headed for the refrigerator, grabbing the bottle from Stacy on the way. At seventeen months Stacy was still very attached to her bottle. It was her security, and I hadn't had the heart to wean her from it.

Tonya was rocking on the bed beside the door. I kissed her one last time. "Steve, take good care of the girls for me," I called.

"I will," he said, not even looking up from the television. Greg distracted Stacy with the bottle while I slipped out the door.

I was puzzled to find George sitting in the passenger seat when I came out.

"You want me to drive?"

"I've got a little bit of a headache," he answered. "Do you mind?"

"Not at all," I said, jumping in behind the wheel. "It's just that you hardly ever want me to."

We pulled out of the driveway and headed out into the fog, leaving our four healthy children all alone.

Chapter 7

Tragedy

Stephen and Mary had just served their last four customers when George and I stopped by Poor Jim's to see if they were ready to join us at the Legion. I helped Mary clean tables and reset them for tomorrow while Stephen and George stepped outside for a cigarette. Stephen never smoked in the kitchen.

The two dining couples ate leisurely, not the least bit concerned that they were holding us up. Mary and I had long since finished setting the tables, and now it was getting late. George and I decided to go on ahead, promising to save Stephen and Mary a seat when we got there.

We reached the community building just before the first game was to start. I spied the auxiliary president in the crowd and went over to explain why I wasn't able to make it to the meeting last night. We quickly bought our cards and found a table in the center row. Stephen and Mary joined us in the middle of the first game.

It was a typical night. The four of us weren't winning a thing. But we'd go back to the restaurant afterward for a late snack and jam session to figure out that elusive winning formula. Stephen said he'd just received a booklet in the mail he'd sent for on how to win at Bingo.

I came close to winning the fifth game, and my excitement overflowed as I busily daubed the numbers with my big red Bingo dauber.

Stephen reached across the table and daubed my arm to tease me. I shot him a silly sneer and we all snickered under our breath.

A few numbers later George reached over and got Stephen's arm in retaliation. Mary reached across and daubed George's arm, and I reached over and did the same to Mary. We all laughed at the bright red quarter-size dots on our arms. People around us were starting to stare, which made us giggle more.

Just after ten o'clock, I noticed a man enter the building and whisper to the woman at the counter. The woman looked over at us, and then came our way. The man waited at the door. He looked very upset.

"There's someone here who wants to talk to you," she whispered in George's ear.

George stood to follow her, motioning for me to stay and watch his cards. When they reached the door, the man led George outside. A few minutes later George stepped back inside and signaled for me to join him. Now George looked upset, too. I left everything on the table and joined him immediately.

"Come on. We've gotta get home," he said. He took me by the arm and led me out the door.

"Why?" I questioned, suddenly frightened by the frozen terror in his face. "George, what's the matter?"

"I don't know. But we're going home."

There were people gathered outside. They all appeared quite upset but none of them would tell us why. The man who summoned George outside was crying; I heard someone call him Pete. George was pulling me toward the car. I wanted to know what was going on!

"Pete, what happened?" I yelled, hoping to get an answer by knowing his name, as if it were some secret password.

He trembled uncontrollably, and I wondered if he was even going to be able to speak. My eyes pierced him like a knife.

He finally blurted it out. "Something terrible. Please, just go home." He turned away from me so I wouldn't see his tears.

An urgency gripped me. Something was wrong with the kids. It had to be. I ran to keep up with George. As we headed for our car, Stephen and Mary stepped out of the building.

"Are you their friends?" I heard Pete ask them. "Because if you are, you'd better go with them. They're going to need you."

George had the engine running before I could close my door. We pulled out of the parking lot with a screech, leaving a trail of rubber on the pavement.

That first ten miles was the longest in my life. We didn't talk at all, too afraid to verbalize our fears. George leaned forward against the steering wheel to see through the fog and drove as fast as he dared.

All the while, I wondered what in the world could have happened. An accident of some kind. A fire perhaps. One of the kids was hit by a car. The hospital called about Stephanie. I had no idea what awaited us at home. I only knew it was so serious it made strangers cry.

We pulled onto Lake Road EE and headed up the last three miles. I craned to look across the lake where we could usually see our house standing on the hill in the peaceful glow of the yard light. But tonight the whole hilltop was afire with flashing red emergency lights. I panicked.

"Oh my God, George. What's going on?"

He didn't answer.

Around the last bend to home a police car blocked our way. A patrolman stood in the road and waved for us to stop.

"What in the hell is this?" George yelled, striking the steering wheel with the palm of his hand. He pulled to a stop and rolled down the window part way. The patrolman leaned against the car.

"Sorry, folks," he said politely. "But this road has been closed to any unnecessary traffic. May I ask where you're going tonight?"

George scowled at him through gritted teeth. "Look, my name is George Swift, and I live down here. Something's wrong with my kids, and I'm going through."

He forced the car into gear and sped away. The patrolman did nothing to stop us.

Around the bend, I was not prepared for what I saw. There was home in full view, standing pink against the flashing lights. Patrol cars and ambulances lined both sides of the road, too many to count quickly. Officers and ambulance attendants were everywhere.

With no place to park, George halted in the middle of the road, leaped from the car, and sprinted to the front porch. A ditch on my side forced me to run around the back of a patrol car. I made it halfway across the yard before two ambulance attendants caught up with me. Each one grabbed an arm and pulled me back.

"Let me go!" I yelled. "Those are my kids in there. I've got to get in there!"

The woman attendant looked at me sympathetically, but the man held even tighter to my arm and wouldn't let go.

Two police officers stopped George at the door before he could get in. One had his service revolver out of its holster and pointed directly at him. It was clear they weren't going to let him in. George held his ground on the front porch. I couldn't hear what he was saying, but he was waving his arms frantically.

"Why don't we go across the street," the woman suggested.

They led me to an ambulance and made me sit down on the back bumper. The back doors were wide open. The two attendants stood guard over me to keep me from running toward the house. It would be useless to try, I reasoned. I was way outnumbered.

I sat there on the cold hard bumper trying to calm down and make some sense out of what was happening. I studied the scenes around me trying to gain some clues. Men and women in uniform were stationed all over the yard. All of them seemed so calm and business-like. But my mind was in turmoil! I was shaking so hard I couldn't control it. I looked toward the house.

George was still on the front porch with the officers. The tall one had put his gun away. Not one light shone inside the house. I noticed that one curtain was propped open in the living room, and I squinted to see inside. As much as I wanted to, I could detect no movement at all.

I looked up at the woman attendant, trying hard to show an air of control. "What happened?" My voice quivered. My eyes pleaded for an answer.

"We don't know," she said quietly.

"Well, where are my kids?" I asked. "Are they in the ambulance?" I spun around, wishing desperately to see them there. I saw only white emptiness.

I turned back to the woman, my teary eyes speaking volumes. "I have a right to know. You must tell me something, anything!"

"They're still in the house," the woman stammered.

Again I looked toward the house. It was pitch black! Nobody was in there trying to help my kids. If they were hurt, they wouldn't just leave them in there all alone. A doctor would be in there, or they'd be in an ambulance on their way to the hospital.

If they were okay, why wouldn't they let them come out to me? I wrestled with all the options, trying to put together a logical reason for their being in there all alone in the dark. And everyone else standing out here? There was only one reason, and it just couldn't be true. Oh God, no, it couldn't be true.

I turned to the attendants and, in almost a whisper, I said, "They're all dead, aren't they."

The two attendants bowed their heads to the ground, afraid to look at me. The man kicked a rock with his shoe. The woman sighed, and the word was barely audible.

"Yes."

I closed my eyes against the pain of my heart crumbling. "No!" My mind wanted to cry out. "This isn't happening!" But it would do no good. The answer had been "Yes," and it was too late to change it.

George was coming toward me now, flanked by the two officers. I rose to my feet and met him in the middle of the road.

"George," I cried, allowing the tears of rage to spill out. "They're all dead! They're all dead!"

"I know," he said, holding me tight against his chest. "Somebody broke in and shot 'em."

"Shot them!' I cried in hysterics. "George, why would anybody want to shoot the kids? They never hurt anybody!"

"I don't know," he said. His body was so numb with shock that he couldn't even feel the rage.

But I did. I began to say crazy things, trying to turn back the clock and change what had happened.

"Why didn't they go next door?" I babbled as fast as the words would come. "Nobody was home there. Why didn't they just steal everything we own? They could have it all. I don't want any of it. It's useless to me!

"Why didn't they just lock the kids in the closet? Why didn't they kidnap the kids? At least we could pay a ransom and get them back.

"Why did they have to kill them? They didn't gain anything by that. Nobody gained anything by killing them! Good God, George, why did they have to kill them?"

I buried my face in George's chest, heaving and shivering in the cold. The man attendant wrapped his jacket around my shoulders to warm me. But George said nothing. He was completely numb.

* * *

Stephen and Mary drove up in their Chevy Blazer, and Mary ran straight to me and grabbed me. "Oh Joy, I'm so sorry," she cried.

Stephen laid his hand on George's shoulder. "George, are you all right?" he asked, at a loss for what to say or do.

George stared blankly at the dark house standing like a still and silent tomb. "I can't believe this is happening," he whispered.

"I'll be right back," Stephen said. "We need some help."

Stephen ran over to one of the officers and asked him to radio in a call to his pastor. Don Turner was pastor of the Lakeland Baptist Church as well as the tiny summer church next door. We'd only met him once before, when he'd heard of Stephanie's illness and brought over a box of food and a check for a hundred dollars to help us out. Within twenty minutes Pastor Turner stood beside us in the road.

Robin and Lucky bounded out of the woods and jumped up to greet us. I let go of George and bent down to hug them.

"What happened, Robin?" I demanded, shaking her by the collar. "Why didn't you stop it?"

Her innocent canine eyes looked so sad and confused. If only she could tell me what happened before the police came. I hugged her tighter, guilty that I accused her. Did she know she'd never see Steve again?

An hour passed and nothing happened. Everyone just stood in the road and waited. We didn't know for what. I wanted them to bring the kids out, but nobody made any moves to indicate they were going to.

In our hurry to get home we'd left our cigarettes on the Bingo table, and now all four of us were needing one to steady us. Stephen went in search of a pack from one of the attendants.

I looked across the yard at all the signs of children living here. Greg's bicycle parked beside the front porch. The swing set in the side yard, its white plastic swings swaying in the cool night breeze. The three Easter ducks resting quietly in their pen.

I remembered the dead rabbit, the missing ducks and even the hundreds of tiny holes in the side of the house caused by a shotgun blast before we even bought the house and moved in. We'd had no clue as to the cause of these incidents. They were mysteries we shrugged off when no answers came.

But how could the children be gone from this place? This was a mystery I could not accept. My entire life had been built around them.

An officer approached us to ask if we'd come to the police station and answer some questions.

"Oh no," I announced belligerently. "I'm not leaving here until you bring my kids out." I turned and stared at the house.

Until I saw the bodies, I would not accept that they were dead. They could keep me from going into the house. But sooner or later they'd have to bring the kids out.

The officer tried again and again to get us to go with him. But I'd made up my mind and wild horses wouldn't drag me away. It didn't matter to me how much time passed. I had no place else to go but here.

Finally, the officer took Pastor Turner aside to ask if he had any ideas. Don sauntered over and stood close to me.

"You know, there are relatives that need to be notified," he mentioned in a smooth persuasive voice. "We need you to tell us who they are and how to get a hold of them."

Immediately my mind focused on the boys' mother. "Oh my God...Jean," I wailed. "How are we going to tell her?" I grew frantic.

I looked to George for an answer but he just shook his head, unable to make a decision. Don offered to drive us to the police station to make the calls.

"Okay," I agreed. "But you must promise to bring us back here just as soon as we're done."

Stephen wasn't aware the police wanted us at the station. "George," he offered, "We can use the phone at the restaurant if you prefer."

I seized the opportunity immediately. "Yes, George, Poor Jim's is closer. We'll get back quicker."

George nodded in agreement.

The officer seemed very unhappy about our choice until Don took him aside to talk in private.

"Okay, we're going to Poor Jim's," Don said. "But, George, you're in no condition to drive. I'll drive you and Joy there, and Stephen and Mary can follow in their car."

We climbed into the back seat of Don's car, unaware of the secret plan he had with the police.

* * *

When we reached Poor Jim's I jumped out of the car and headed straight for the door, anxious to get the calls made and get back to the house. Mary had the keys and followed quickly to let me in. Her parents were waiting in the parking lot and followed us in. Evidently, Mary had contacted them by C.B. radio and asked them to come.

As soon as we got inside, I started asking all the "whys" all over again. Don Turner came in and grabbed me by the shoulders. He spun me around and looked me square in the eye.

"Joy, you've got to be strong now. We need you. George has just broken down outside. He's in the parking lot throwing up."

"I gotta go to him," I said, struggling to free myself from his grasp.

He held me tighter and pulled me back. "No. Stephen is with him. We need you to give us the addresses of the people you want us to contact. We'll find ministers to go to their homes. This is not something you tell someone over the phone."

I stood up straight and became strong, just as I'd done for Stephanie. "I'm bigger than this. I'm not going to be stupid and lose my head. I can be strong!" I gave Don the addresses of Jean, my parents and George's mother. He made the necessary calls to send ministers with the horrible news.

George came in looking very pale and drained. He collapsed into a chair and stared blankly at the wall. I sat beside him thumbing a napkin, folding it in different ways to keep occupied. I grew impatient and asked why we couldn't head back to the house.

"We'll wait just a little longer," Don said, stalling for more time.

My patience was wearing thinner. I tore the napkin into tiny pieces and stuffed them into a Styrofoam cup. Then I destroyed the cup as well.

A patrol car pulled into the parking lot and I jumped up to greet the officer. "Let's go," he said.

At last, we were heading back to the house.

George and I rode in the back seat of the patrol car while Don and the Pyeatts followed along in their own vehicles. We drove in silence for the first ten miles until we passed the turn-off to our house. I leaned over the seat and pointed to the turn-off.

"You missed the turn back there," I said.

The patrolman nodded his head slowly. "I was told to take you to the police station."

I flew into a rage again. "They lied to us!" I screamed. "They said they'd take us back to the house."

George pulled me down on the seat and held me tight. "They've got to ask us some questions," he said. "Then they'll bring us back."

I clung to George with all I had. I'd been deceived long enough. I wanted honesty. I would answer their questions. But I wanted mine answered, too. I felt hollow and empty inside. If someone had hollered down my throat just then it would have echoed right back at them. We settled down for the long ride to the police station.

Chapter 8

Interrogation

I paced the length of the front office of the police station, my rage growing with each step. They had whisked George away for questioning as soon as we arrived. He'd been gone for over three hours now, and the way I was being treated by the police, George was the only one I trusted anymore.

Stephen and Mary had waited with me for an hour before they were taken in for questioning. But they had come out long ago and gone home to take care of their children.

Don Turner sat silently in the padded desk chair and watched my anger boil. I had been told nothing. I only knew that someone broke into the house and shot the kids, and my hatred for whomever could have done such a thing could not have been more intense. I wanted to kill them for what they did to my babies.

Don's quiet demeanor raked at my nerves. I couldn't stand it any longer.

"Why can't I find the ones who did this and string 'em up and shoot 'em a thousand times?" the words spewed from my mouth. "Doesn't the Bible say, 'An eye for an eye'?"

Don folded his hands on the desk and looked at me seriously. "Joy, you should feel sorry for whoever did this to your children. Someday they'll feel the wrath of God."

"Sorry!" I screamed at him. "Why should I feel sorry for them? They're murderers! What could my children possibly have done to provoke them to kill? I feel sorry for my children. I feel sorry for me!"

Don sat back and fell silent once more.

"Prove it to me from the Bible, Mister Minister," I thought as I stomped back and forth. "Tell me what the Bible really says, because right now I want to know how God feels about what has happened to my children. My precious children. My sweet precious babies." I fell against the concrete wall and sobbed, the anger giving way to emptiness.

The phone rang, and Don spoke for several minutes before handing the receiver to me. "It's your father," he said.

I took the phone and pressed it to my ear. "Dad?"

"Honey, what happened?"

"Oh Dad," I whimpered, as the tears burned in my sockets. "Somebody broke into the house and shot the kids. They're all dead!"

"Well, where were you and George?" he asked, almost accusingly.

"We were at the American Legion playing Bingo." The excuse sounded so lame, so stupid. Our children were dying, and we were playing games.

Dad's voice changed, more comforting now. "Do you want Mom and me to come down? Do you need us?"

"Yeah, Dad, I do. Please come."

"We're coming, Sweetheart. Just hang on."

Dad hung up the phone and turned to Mom and Father Yonkman, the Episcopal priest who had come to their apartment to deliver the news.

"They didn't do it," he said. "I know my daughter, and she isn't lying. Neither she nor George has anything to do with the children's deaths."

"Is there anything I can do?" Father Yonkman asked.

"Thanks, but no," Dad answered him. "We're heading down to Camdenton right away."

Mom rushed toward the bedroom. "I'll pack a suitcase."

"No!" Dad called her back. "There isn't time. We'll buy what we need when we get there." He kicked the wall in disgust. "God, why did I ever get rid of my service revolver?"

Mom looked at him fearfully. "Why do you need a gun?"

"Because if George and Joy didn't kill the kids, we don't know who did. What if they come back gunning for George and Joy? How can I protect them without a weapon?"

Mom and Dad flew out the door, completely forgetting about my eighteen-year-old sister Dawn, who sat on the edge of her bed clutching a Bible as Father Yonkman broke the news.

"Please, God, no," she whispered while hearing the priest's words.

"I have a message from Camdenton, Missouri, about Steve, Greg, Tonya and Stacy Swift," he said. "Apparently they've been shot. Their parents are being held for questioning in the killings."

Dawn flung the Bible across the room. "There is no God!" she cried. "There is no God!"

* * *

At four o'clock in the morning, George emerged from the door across the hall, and just as quickly I was ordered to follow the police officer who led him out. I had no time to ask George why they had taken his shirt from him, and no time to dwell on it.

The police officer led me to an interrogation room and shut the door.

"Mrs. Swift, you have the right to remain silent," he began. "Anything you say can and will be used against you in a court of law. You have the right to an attorney..." He finished reading me my Miranda rights. "Do you understand what I have just said?" he asked.

"Yes," I answered, confused. Having grown up with police officers, I could recite the Miranda rights word-for-word. But now it was different.

"No, wait. I don't understand. I mean, I can understand why the murderer needs an attorney, but why do I need one? I...I do know an attorney. Do you think I need one?"

"Mrs. Swift, that's up to you," the officer said. "You have the right to have an attorney present during questioning. If you'd like, we'll begin the questioning and if, at any time, you would like to stop, we will do so until an attorney can be present."

"Okay." I sat down, still confused.

The officer lit a cigarette and offered me one. He started out by asking me questions about the kids—their names and ages; whether they had any sores, injuries or scars; what kind of relationship George and I had with them.

He wanted to know who had been at the house this past week. Friends, salesmen, anybody asking for help? I fully intended to cooperate with him. I wanted the murderers found. Billy had been our only visitor all week. There had been no strangers, no strange phone calls, nothing.

The questions came so fast I barely had time to think. What time did we leave the house tonight? Was there anyone there when we left besides the kids? What took place right before we left?

I told him about the play fight George had with the boys, arguing and wrestling over whether it was our turn to go out. The officer looked worried.

"Does George believe in corporal punishment?" he asked. "Did George beat the children before you left?"

I had to laugh. George never punished those kids! I was the one who dished out the discipline. He never even spanked them.

"When you left home, did you go directly to the Legion Hall?"

He took notes and looked concerned when I told him we'd stopped at Poor Jim's, and George and Stephen Pyeatt had gone outside for a cigarette.

"Did they leave the restaurant at any time?"

I told him no. They stayed right on the porch.

"Are you sure there is no short-cut, no back way from Poor Jim's to your house? No way they could have slipped out and come back?"

"No way," I shook my head. I didn't like this questioning. "You don't really believe George would have anything to do with killing his own kids." The very idea was preposterous.

"Mrs. Swift, we have to follow every lead. How long were you at the restaurant?"

"Twenty...twenty-five minutes?" I guessed.

I bummed cigarettes from him until he was out. He left the room momentarily and returned with a new pack. The questions resumed.

"Do you keep any alcohol or drugs in the house?"

"George drinks beer," I said honestly. "There's a six-pack in the fridge. And a half a bottle of wine," I remembered. "We just celebrated our anniversary four days ago." My roses still stood in the middle of the kitchen table.

"Does George keep any guns in the house?"

"Yes," I told him. "I think he has three pistols and five or six rifles or shotguns. Most of them I've never even seen out of their cases."

"Have you fired a gun in the past twenty-four hours?" he continued.

"No, sir. I've only shot a gun once in my whole life, two years ago at my grandfather's farm. I missed the whole fifty-five gallon drum I was aiming at."

The officer rose from his chair. "Then you won't mind submitting to a powder residue test."

He escorted me into another room and pulled a residue kit from a cabinet. He fumbled with the test kit, ripping the plastic bag open and reaching for the rubber gloves inside.

He parted the fingers of my right hand and rubbed the wet cotton thoroughly across my palms and fingertips. He repeated the procedure on my left hand, then sealed the swab in a plastic bag and labeled it for the lab.

The officer then pulled out an ink pad and card and took my fingerprints. He passed me a wadded-up paper towel to wipe away the ink from my fingers. I rubbed my fingers vigorously, but most of the ink stayed on.

He called a woman bailiff into the room and told her to take me into the restroom for a strip-search. I had no idea why, but I cooperated. It was the most demeaning thing I'd ever had to do. When I told her I had to go to the bathroom she watched me go.

We went back to the interrogation room where the questions continued. The officer wanted to see the tread on my shoes. When I asked him why, he told me they had found prints under a window where the killers apparently fled.

I told him about George's kangaroo-hide boots that Greg had thrown away just before we left, just in case they needed to see the tread on those. The officer really looked concerned then. Where was the dump and exactly where did Greg throw them? Only Greg knew, and he was dead.

* * *

Down the hall, George was being held in a room alone with a guard placed at the door. He had asked to use the restroom several times and been told he couldn't. He'd needed to go during his own strip-search but refused to do it in front of the officer. That was hours ago. He peeked his head out and asked the guard again. The answer was still no.

George had been very cooperative up till then. Having served on the police force for eight years, he knew the procedure and understood that we had to be eliminated as suspects. He'd answered all their questions courteously, and even kept his cool when they'd taken his shirt to test a chili stain they thought was blood.

He remained calm when they found a massive six-inch bruise on his right calf, and asked him if he sustained it in a scuffle with the kids. Perhaps one of them managed a swift kick as he was killing them. George told them the truth. A boat hit him there while he was pulling it up to a trailer that day, but they didn't want to believe him.

They'd taken mug shots of him, but only after George showed the young officer how to use the camera. He even had to remind the officer to put on the rubber gloves before doing his powder residue test, so the officer's fingers wouldn't contaminate George's test.

Some of it had been funny. But after six-and-a-half hours George's patience was wearing thin. The numbness that took over at the house was being replaced with anger. All he wanted to do was go to the bathroom.

George took a deep breath and headed out the door. The guard rose clumsily from his chair and grabbed for his gun. George turned to face him.

"Look, you can shoot me in the back if you want to," he said. "But I'm going to the bathroom."

The guard followed him in, watched him go, then escorted him back to the windowless room and closed the door.

George paced the floor like a caged lion, tapping his teeth together to control his impatience. He hated windowless rooms. The pack of cigarettes he'd been given was nearly empty. He lit one, then another, then a third. He opened the door and peeked outside. The guard was nowhere in sight.

Across the hall, he could see several officers eating doughnuts and drinking coffee, their arms crossed seriously as they exchanged information. It must have been early morning. The first rays of sunlight were pouring in through the tiny window beside the front entry.

He'd heard the delivery boy pass by an hour ago, and learned later that the refreshments had been donated by a local bakery to help the officers who would spend long hours in search of the murderers. George felt he could use some coffee himself and fully intended to get some.

He stepped out into the hall and walked toward the front office where I had been taken when we first arrived. Just then the guard spied his escape and ran to intercept him, sloshing the fresh cup of coffee he had just retrieved for himself.

George stood defiantly and pushed his nose into the officer's face. "How can you lock me up in that room and forget me?" He bellowed before the officer could say a word. "I'm not going back in there!"

Don Turner heard his insults echoing down the hall and ran out to grab him by the shoulders.

"Calm down now, George," he ordered. "You're too upset."

"I don't want to calm down," he yelled. "I have every right to be upset." He could smell coffee on Don's breath.

"You're all sitting around having coffee and doughnuts, and you don't give a damn that my kids are out there dead! Did anyone think to offer me any coffee or doughnuts? Huh? All I'm asking for is a little bit of respect."

He turned to the officer, who gazed sheepishly at his half-filled cup. Nobody apologized or offered to get him a cup.

"I've had enough!" George demanded. "I want out of here. Where's my wife?"

"Your wife has been taken in for questioning," the officer said. "It'll be a while before she's through. You can go on into the front office and wait with Pastor Turner. Your in-laws are in there, too."

George lead the way to the office. "They better find the ones who did this," he threatened. "And when they do, they better give them the death penalty for killing my kids."

Don Turner stopped him in his tracks. "George, that's no way to talk," he admonished. "Whoever did this is going to feel the wrath of God. You should get down on your knees and pray for forgiveness for whoever did this."

"Pray for them!" he laughed with a vengeance. "I'll save my prayers for those who deserve them." The murderers could rot in hell.

* * *

Mom wriggled in her chair impatiently. She and Dad had waited for over an hour before George finally joined them. Now another hour was nearly gone, and I still hadn't emerged.

"When is Joy being brought out?" she asked. "I need to see her."

"It can't be much longer," Don said. "I'm worried about how she's handling all this, though. She's carrying far too much anger for her own good."

"What do you think we should do?" Mom asked.

"I called the clinic, and the doctor suggested she be brought in for a tranquilizer to help her settle down."

"I don't think she'll go without a fight," Dad piped up. "I know my daughter. She inherited my temper." George chuckled and nodded his head.

"She might go," Mom said, "If I tell her it's for me." A plan was quickly put together.

After three hours of questioning, the officer took me back to the front office, then ducked out to join the other officers across the hall for coffee and doughnuts. One pulled the curtain across the interior window so we couldn't watch them eating.

I went over and hugged Mom to comfort her, then bummed a cigarette from Dad. A chain smoker, I knew he'd bring plenty. George and I usually didn't smoke that much, a pack a day between us. But tonight I couldn't let go of one.

George shivered from the cold buttons of his overalls against his bare chest. I handed him the ambulance jacket I'd been given the night before. How could they possible think we'd killed our own kids? What kind of parents did they think we were?

The big clock on the wall read half past seven. I shook my head in disgust. We'd been here all night and the only clue I had after all this time was that the killers left footprints under a window. Now that the questioning was over, I was ready for someone to take me back to the house.

Mom piped up. "I think I need to go get something to calm me down," she said. "Joy, would you go with me?"

I answered without hesitation. "Mom, I can't leave right now. I have to find out what happened to the kids."

"But, honey," Mom pleaded. "I need you with me."

I rolled my eyes impatiently and looked over at George for a way out, the way the kids always did when they wanted him to fix things.

"Just go," he surrendered. "They'll bring you right back." He walked away from me and leaned against the wall. There was no sense in fighting them. They would push until they won.

So much for support, I thought, as I half-heartedly followed Don and Mom out the door. If Mom felt she needed something to calm her down, that was fine. But I didn't need any artificial drug to keep me strong. I had enough strength for two people right now. I could have taken on a lion barehanded. But I wasn't prepared for the sight of the school buses going by.

"Oh God, the buses," I cried, my legs turning to rubber underneath me. Mom rushed to steady me.

"Today's picture day, Mom," I whimpered. "I'll never get another picture of the kids again. Never!"

A nurse met us at the back door of the clinic. She recognized me from Steph's visit a few weeks before. She asked how Steph was doing, and I told her they'd found cancer.

"That's hard news to take," she said, thinking that was the reason we'd come.

"I know," I said. "But last night, somebody murdered my other four. The healthy ones. They killed the healthy ones."

"Oh my God," the nurse cried. She ran to get the doctor.

The doctor calmly prepared a hypodermic and turned to me. "Do you want this in your arm or your hip?" he asked.

"Oh, no," I said. "I'm fine. Mom's the one who wants the shot."

"It's just to calm you down," he persuaded.

"I don't need to calm down. I have to find out what happened to my kids. I've got to know how they were killed."

They all worked to convince me it would be easier if I just took the shot.

"It won't put me to sleep, will it? I can't go to sleep. I've got to get back to the house."

They promised me it wouldn't put me to sleep.

"All right, all right, just do it so I can get back," I demanded.

"Do you want that in your arm or your hip?" the doctor asked again.

"My arm," I pointed. "It's faster." I didn't have time to half undress for the stupid thing. I rolled up my sleeve for the shot.

"Okay, Mom," I said when he finished. "It's your turn."

"Oh, I don't need anything," Mom answered sweetly.

I glared at her. My own mother deceived me. I wanted to hit her. Everybody was lying to me! I didn't need that shot. I didn't!

* * *

We returned to the police station and were ordered back to the front office, the one I now called the monkey cage. With that big glass wall overlooking the entry, everybody who entered the building could see us. I felt like an animal on display.

Eight o'clock passed, then nine. We paced, we sat and we waited, smoking like chimneys from the carton of cigarettes Dad brought along. By now I trusted no one, and wasn't in any particular mood to be compliant anymore. Everybody kept his distance and let me seethe it out.

Don left to go talk to the officers across the hall. I finally sat down in the padded desk chair and rested my head on the desk. I was furious the shot was trying to put me to sleep, and was fighting the tranquilizer with everything I had.

At half past nine, the reporters burst through the front door and filled the hallway like a swarm of bees. They completely ignored us, focusing their attention instead on the deputy who came out to give the report. I noticed he looked awfully young to be a deputy. He couldn't have been out of his twenties.

The reporters hushed as he raised his hands to speak. I jumped from the desk chair and pressed my ear to the glass.

The deputy was telling the reporters that the younger boy was found in the yard, apparently running away from the house, when he was gunned down.

"George, they found Greg in the yard!" I cried out in horror. "He was running away!"

George ran to my side to get closer. We pressed against the glass to hear more. The deputy said Steve was found under a couch, and one of the girls was in a bed. The other girl was on the floor.

"Which bed, which girl?" My mind reeled at the fuzzy details. Why can't they tell us?

A reporter asked how old the children were.

"The two boys were twelve and fourteen, I think," The deputy offered. "The two little girls were, I don't know... one and...two maybe."

I exploded in a ball of fury. I pounded my fist against the glass, outraged by the deputy's incompetence. "She's four! Damn you! She's four!" my screams penetrated the glass.

The reporters turned to stare in astonishment, their mini-action cameras rolling. George pulled me away from the glass and back against the wall. I sobbed in his arms.

"She's four, George," I whimpered. "Her birthday is eleven days away. Don't let them take away the few years she had."

"I know, Punkin," George soothed through his own tears.

We listened as the deputy gave the complete names of the children to the reporters.

"My God," George cried. "I've got relatives that haven't even been told and he's giving them names!"

The reporters turned to go and the deputy ducked back into an inner office. The silent waiting continued.

I returned to the desk to rest my head, which was whirling from the tranquilizer. George smoked a cigarette and paced some more. Mom stayed in her chair against the wall, unable to atone for deceiving me at the clinic.

Dad crushed his cigarette out on the floor and leaned against the wall to steady himself. He began to shudder, trying to hold back his tears, but they burst forward in an avalanche of uncontrollable sobs. George went over to him and put his arms around him.

"I'm sorry, George." Dad wiped his eyes against the back of his hand. "I came down here to be strong for you and Joy, and now here I am crying like a baby."

"Hey, we're all going to cry," George assured him. "That's why we're all here. To comfort each other when one of us breaks down."

Dad buried his face in the ambulance jacket and let the tears come. "I loved my grandkids so much," he cried. "So very much."

* * *

The young deputy entered the office and walked up to the desk where I was resting. I waited until he was close enough, then lunged from the chair and grabbed him by the collar.

"How dare you tell those reporters, those strangers, about our kids before you tell us!" I screamed.

The deputy went wide-eyed with shock. Dad and George rushed to pull me off of him.

"We've been here all night," I raved, kicking to be released from their grip. "We've answered all their questions, and they haven't answered even one of ours!"

The deputy straightened his collar. "Look, I'm sorry," he said. "Tell me what you want to know."

"You should be sorry," George bellowed, pointing an accusing finger at him. "You told the newspapers and TV the kids' names and I've got relatives that don't even know! How could you do that?"

The deputy stood there, not knowing what to say.

"I want out of here now!" George demanded.

The deputy stepped back. "We're going to get you out of here pretty quick. We've arranged to put you up in a motel here in town. You are free to go. But you must not leave town until we notify you."

He turned to Mom and Dad.

"Mr. and Mrs. Kirkham, we've arranged for an adjoining room for you."

Mom nodded her thanks.

I still wanted to go back to the house. But the deputy informed us the bodies had already been moved to the county morgue. The house was sealed until an investigation crew from Jefferson City was finished collecting evidence. It would probably be another day before we could get anything out of it.

Ten hours after arriving at the police station, we walked out the front door without an escort. We piled into Mom and Dad's Volkswagen hatchback and headed for the Lan-O-Lakes Motel.

Chapter 9

Don't Tell Steph

Stephanie lay in her hospital bed half awake watching a game show on television. She wondered why her dad hadn't come to get her. She had called Debbie the night before and asked her to go to our house and tell him she could come home for the weekend. Like last weekend, she'd wanted him to come early so she could make it a long weekend home.

The nurses came in that morning to say her dad might not make it in during the day. They hadn't said why. But she was fairly depressed. Here the doctors okayed her release, and her dad couldn't even find the time to take her home. Didn't he realize how lonely she was in this anesthetic place so far from family?

She felt much better than she did the previous Friday and had packed her own suitcase to be ready. If only there was a phone at home she'd call and find out why Dad hadn't come. She was too busy with her own thoughts to give the game show her complete attention when a news bulletin flashed on the television screen.

"Two suspects were taken into custody this morning in connection with the slaying of four Camdenton children who were found brutally murdered in their home on Highway EE while their parents were attending an American Legion function."

Stephanie sat up in bed. "That's our road," she thought, suddenly alert and listening. The report continued.

"The children have been identified as members of the George Swift family."

"No!" she cried. She watched horrified as gurneys carried her sheet-covered siblings from her home. Steve's sneakered foot dangled lifelessly from under the sheet.

"The two men were taken into custody as they docked their fishing boat a few miles downstream of the Swifts' home. The police said they were acting on a tip that one of the men disliked children. The police were careful to point out that the men were simply being questioned and have not been charged."

"No!" Stephanie's screams echoed down the corridor. She pounded her fists against the bed furiously. "No!"

Two nurses sprinted down the hall and barrelled into Stephanie's room. They grabbed Steph's arms and held her down.

"Steph, what's the matter?" one of them cried.

Stephanie struggled to be freed. "They're all dead!" she shrieked, pointing to the screen. "They're all dead!" She collapsed into the nurse's arms and wept uncontrollably.

The nurses stared at each other over her shoulder. George had called that morning and asked them not to tell Stephanie until we could be with her. They hadn't even thought to take the television out of the room.

"I want my dad," Stephanie demanded hoarsely. "Where's my dad?"

* * *

Not knowing who killed the kids, we kept the curtains drawn, and the motel room was dark and dismal. The police had released us under Mom and Dad's supervision, but they wouldn't let us leave town to be with Stephanie. I prayed that she didn't know yet.

The television was on constantly to catch any bulletins. We watched as the kids were carried from the house, and I cried when I saw Steve's foot dangling out. We wondered who the two men were that police picked up for questioning. Why would they walk in and kill the kids for no reason? It didn't make sense.

Dad and George had slipped out early to get a newspaper. The headline of the *Springfield News-Leader* read: "Four Camden County Children Found Slain." The article offered the first clues about what happened while we were gone.

Mom tried to make me believe the kids were all asleep when they were killed, and they didn't feel the pain when they were shot. But the newspaper told us otherwise.

It said that Tonya was found in our bed. Steve was halfway under the couch, and Stacy lay on the living room floor with a bottle in her hand. Greg was found in the backyard ten yards from the house. Apparently they had all been gunned down as they fled.

The paper said there was no sign of forcible entry. Both of the doors were unlocked when police arrived. The kids were all found fully clothed and had not been bound. Police had no motive, no weapon, and no witnesses.

It said further that a girl who sometimes babysits for us had come to the house to deliver a message and found the children dead. We learned from the police that it was Debbie, delivering Steph's message that she could come home for the weekend.

The article was far from accurate, though. Names, ages and other details were incorrect. They called our house "a pink framed cottage." It wasn't pink. It was brown. Cocoa or hot chocolate brown. It only looked pink because of all the emergency lights flashing around it. George was too much of a man to ever live in a pink house!

In spite of the inaccuracies, we did our best to try to piece together what happened in the house that night. There just weren't enough clues.

Two policemen came to tell us they needed someone to identify the bodies at the morgue. I quickly volunteered for the job. At last I could see my babies!

After some argument I lost out, and Dad got to go. Dad intended to use the opportunity to find out just how the kids were killed, and because he had a trained eye, George wanted him to go. There were certain things Dad would be able to tell that I wouldn't.

I peered out the window as they left in the patrol car. I envied them. Why couldn't anybody understand I needed to be with the kids? I went into the other room and cried alone.

Dad tried hard to swallow his grandfatherly feelings and look at the bodies as pieces of evidence. A patrolman stood at his side as he identified the children. He would not let himself cry in front of a fellow officer.

When he returned, Dad said that by all indications Greg had died from a single bullet wound to the head.

"It looks like he was shot in the eye," he said, a tinge of disbelief in his voice. "But he looked peaceful. He probably died before he even hit the ground."

He said the side of Greg's face was plastered with blood and grass. The rest of him looked untouched.

But the other three suffered multiple wounds. Tonya's and Stacy's heads were partially blown open by the blasts. Steve's chest was riddled with bullets. All three of the children found inside had a look of terror frozen on their faces. It went over and over in my mind. Did they call for me as they were dying?

By the time Dad returned, the injection I'd been given was taking control. I lay down on the bed to clear my head, and fell into a deep sleep.

George and Dad slipped out to a clothing store to get us each a change of clothes. George never did get his shirt back from the police, and none of us had a thing except what we had on.

Don phoned the store clerk and explained the situation, and Dad was able to get the clothes at a discount. He paid for them with a credit card. They picked up the newspapers on the way back to the motel.

I awoke hours later to the sound of voices in the adjoining room. By now it was early evening. It surprised me that I had slept so soundly. I was always the last one in the house to fall asleep. It was not unusual for me to still be wide awake at three o'clock in the morning when the baby cried or one of the kids coughed in the night.

I shook my head to clear it and got up to rejoin the others. That tranquilizer the doctor gave me must have been mighty strong. I picked up the evening newspaper. We were front page news again.

The article said that seventeen shots were accounted for, twelve of which were in the children. Steve had been shot four times in the head and chest. Greg was shot once in the left eye. Tonya was shot four times in the head and chest and suffered a superficial knife wound to the chest. Stacy was shot three times in the head and chest at such a close range that it left powder burns. What a horrible way to die.

Mom called relatives on our side of the family, and George called relatives on his. His mom was traveling to Kansas City in the morning from her home in Manhattan, Kansas. She would begin making arrangements for burial at Mount Moriah.

"Get the plots as close to Dad as you can," George instructed. "And go ahead and buy a fifth one for Stephanie. I want to make sure she has a place beside them."

Don wanted to know what we planned to do once the house was released, suggesting we assign power of attorney to a trusted friend to remove our furniture and personal belongings. We had already made up our minds that we would not return to the house to live.

We decided to ask Bob and Doris because they could enlist the help of the entire American Legion to pack up all our stuff. The job was just too big for any one person.

They came to the motel that evening to discuss the details. Everything was to be put into storage until we could find another place to live. All of the children's toys and clothes were to be kept.

I made sure they knew to be careful not to throw away even a scribbled piece of paper just in case it was one of Tonya's drawings. And to be on the lookout for a macaroni necklace Tonya and I had strung together a few days before.

Since Tonya had been shot in our bed, I didn't want any part of it back. And I didn't want Stacy's high chair and crib. I swore I would never have another baby. It would be like trying to replace the others. And there was no way another child could take their place.

Our three Easter ducks were to be released at lake side to fend for themselves. The resort owners promised to keep an eye on them. The dogs would be kenneled.

Mom took notes of the details and gave them to Bob and Doris to carry out. They assured us that everything would be handled properly.

The man we bought the house from offered to take it back and resell it. The five hundred dollars down payment would be returned in the form of a check to one of six area banks that had set up memorial funds for the kids.

The insurance company assured us they would replace the carpeting and paneling damaged by blood and bullets. But because the house was still livable until repairs could be done, they would not pay for the motel room. It was a stupid policy. How could they possibly expect us to live in a house bathed in our children's blood?

Mom and Dad insisted we stay at their apartment until we could get on our feet. Our cars were taken to the Chevy dealership for storage until we could retrieve them. Nobody felt we were in any condition to drive.

Local businesses set out collection jars, and private clubs and organizations were planning fund raisers to help pay the enormous funeral expenses to come.

So many decisions were being made for us without too much concern for what we wanted. George was in such shock that he didn't seem to mind right then. But I detested the interference in our lives. Every decision was another reminder that the kids were dead. My life was in ruins and I had no idea how it could ever be put back together.

Chapter 10

We Know Who Did It

Corporal Herb Thomas and Officer Larry Miller marched side by side down the hall of the Camdenton Junior High School amidst the whispers and stares of students. Some of them were crying in the halls. Others were quiet and sad.

A female student approached the men in uniform.

"Is it true?" She hugged a notebook to her chest. "Is it true the Swift kids were killed last night?"

"I'm afraid so," the older officer replied. "Did you know the Swift boys?"

"I knew Steve," she said, kicking at her shoe. "Everybody liked Steve. I don't see how anybody could have killed him."

The morning bell brought the students out of their stupor, and the hallways cleared as the crowd filtered away into classrooms. A cloud hung over two of the classes, where empty desks proved that the Swift boys weren't coming back.

Two eighth-grade boys whispered together during first and second hour, trying to hide their nervousness and concentrate on the lesson being taught. Beside them in math and art class was another empty seat, and they knew why.

The police were asking questions from students who rode the bus with Greg and Steve, or those who lived in the area of the murder scene. But Dan and Robbie (not their real names) weren't two of them. If they kept their mouths shut, the police wouldn't talk to them. They sighed with relief when the officers finally left.

But it wasn't right not to tell, and their consciences got the better of them. During third hour, the boys excused themselves and went to the school counselor.

"We know who killed the Swift kids," one of them said.

The counselor summoned the principal, who immediately called the police. The two officers returned to the school and met with Dan and Robbie in private.

"We know who did it," Robbie admitted. "He's been bragging about plans to kill the Swift family for two weeks. He said Mr. Swift owned a bunch of guns and he was going to steal them."

Dan faced Corporal Thomas. "It started out as a plan just to get the guns and some Buck knives he said Mr. Swift owned. But then he started talking about killing anybody that got in his way. He said some guy named Ray was going to help him."

Corporal Thomas quizzed the boys. "Did he say why he wanted the guns?"

"I had a shotgun for sale," Robbie volunteered. "But he didn't have the money to buy it. That's when he started talking about stealing guns from the Swifts."

"Were you two the only ones he talked to about his plan?"

"He told a bunch of us," Dan admitted. "But he talked about it mostly to Robbie and me 'cause we had classes with him. He said if we kept quiet about his plan he was going to give us some of the guns and knives he stole. He was going to sell some of them to other kids."

The corporal sat rigid in his chair. "Did either of you tell the Swifts that someone was threatening to kill them?"

"We didn't know the Swift boys," Robbie said.

"Did you want some of the guns?" Corporal Thomas demanded. "At any time did you offer to buy any of the guns he was going to steal?"

The boys glanced at each other. "No, sir," Robbie said. "We thought he was bragging. Yesterday morning he came to school and said he couldn't wait to open fire on them and get those guns. But we didn't think he'd really do it."

"What's the boy's name?" The Corporal asked, pulling a pad of paper from his pocket. "Is he in school today?"

"No, sir," Robbie said. "He wasn't in math or art class this morning. His name is Billy Dyer."

Corporal Thomas and Juvenile Officer Steve Dorn pulled into the gravel parking space in front of Billy Dyer's cabin. They found that Billy had company, a twenty-year-old man named Ray Richardson, Jr.

Acting on a tip from Robbie and Dan, who said Billy talked about a friend named Ray who was going to help with the crime, they decided to take his friend in for questioning. The two were read their Miranda rights and taken into custody just after five Friday evening.

* * *

We called the police station Friday evening to ask them to send somebody to the motel to talk with us. The two fishermen they'd taken in had been released without any charges filed, which took us back to square one.

The police told reporters they were "questioning everything that moved" in search of clues, but we hadn't heard anything from them. We'd racked our brains all day and thought we might have a few ideas that would help them find the killer. Besides, we were tired of being under house arrest and wanted permission to leave town to be with Stephanie.

The young deputy, Joe Vaughn, arrived just after nine o'clock. Having been on duty for over twenty hours now, his ashen face drooped with fatigue. Mom rushed to clear the newspapers from a chair and politely offered him a seat. He plopped down into it and let out a deep exhausted sigh.

"We took two suspects into custody a few hours ago," the deputy said. "We've got pretty good evidence that they're the ones. The sheriff's being very careful not to make any mistakes. We don't want them let off on a technicality."

At last they sounded like they were on our side.

"So who are they?" George asked.

"Do you know a man named Ray Richardson, Jr.?"

I looked over at George. There was no sign of recognition.

"No. I've never heard the name," George said.

"He lived two miles from your house," Vaughn replied. "In a trailer down by Tiger's Lounge. Evidently Ray Senior's pretty well known in the community."

"Who was the other one?" I asked, trying to find some connection.

"The other suspect is a juvenile," the deputy continued. "Under the law, we can't tell you his name."

"It's Billy, isn't it," George accused. He shot me a quick glance. "Doesn't he live down by Tiger's?"

I nodded. Billy's mother worked at Tiger's Lounge.

Deputy Vaughn turned pink. "I'm sorry. I wish I could tell you." He'd said too much already.

"I know it's him." George said. "He's the only juvenile we know capable of such a thing."

The deputy stood to leave. "I really do wish I could say."

Everyone in the room stood with him. He looked back at me as he turned for the door.

"By the way...Billy. Was his last name Dyer? Or Dryer?"

"It was Dyer," I spouted. "That's it."

The deputy nodded and slipped out the door.

"What was that all about?" George asked after he left.

"During my questioning, Billy's name kept coming up. He's the only visitor we've had all week. But I couldn't for the life of me remember his last name."

* * *

Because Billy was a juvenile, the police were not allowed to question him. Upon arrival at the police station, he was immediately turned over to juvenile authorities.

Camdenton Sheriff Larry Whitten had just returned from an out-of-town fishing trip that afternoon, and Miller County Sheriff Gerald Whittle had been called in to assist in the case. Ray Richardson, Jr. sat in the windowless interrogation room flanked by the two sheriffs.

At first he denied having any knowledge of the killings or the Swift family. But after twenty minutes of questioning, he finally admitted that he was "near" the Swift home about the time of the slaying.

Finally he broke down and made an oral statement, choosing his words carefully to make sure the police understood it was Billy's plan and not his. Yes, he had driven Billy Dyer to the house to steal some guns. He had watched as Billy killed the kids, and fled through an open window when a car pulled into the driveway.

A handwritten statement followed. In his first attempt, he described watching as Billy shot the kids, but neglected to mention Stacy. When the sheriffs questioned him about the baby's death, he quickly added to his statement to accommodate the deletion.

An officer was called in to prepare a typed statement based on the handwritten one. Ray talked his way through it while the sheriffs asked him questions to fill in more details. Afterward, Ray signed it.

The statement offered enough clues to arrest them both for murder. In the wee hours of Saturday morning, Ray was escorted to an empty cell, and the bars clanged shut behind him. In another part of the jail, Billy too sat in a cell.

* * *

I lay in bed that first night without the kids, feeling useless and unneeded, and with too many questions still unanswered. It was the first time in years I only had to worry about putting myself to bed. Even at night, the room was too quiet.

Bedtime had been so much more complicated with the kids. After a drink and potty run, a diaper change for Stacy and the Big Bear's raid, there was often that last minute, "Hey, Dad," to throw in one more word before the lights went out. Oh, how I wanted just one more hug. Just one more day to share with them.

"Why did Billy do it?" I called to George through the darkness. "What did we do to make him want to kill the kids?"

"The window," George said. "I told him if he was man enough to enter my house through the front door, he should be man enough to leave the same way. He killed the kids and then went out that same damn window. I knew he was trouble. From day one, I knew."

Saturday morning the television blared the latest news. Ray E. Richardson, Jr. and the juvenile were being held without bond pending arraignment on Monday. At least now the killers were in custody.

Pastor Turner came late in the morning with coffee and sweet rolls. Normally I would have pounced on the sweet rolls, but I had no appetite to even try them now. In a rare occasion of splurging, I had bought sweet rolls the day the kids were killed.

The kids had asked if they could each have one while we were gone playing Bingo, but I told them to save them for breakfast. Now the precious treat lay untouched on top of the refrigerator of a deserted house.

Since the murderers were in custody, we were free to leave town. But there was no reason to rush off to the hospital now. Stephanie had gone into such shock that she had been taken by ambulance to Jean's house in Kansas City. At least now we worried less about her since she was with her mother, and she'd be there for the funerals.

The house was released, and Don Turner offered to escort Mom and Dad over to retrieve some clothes and personal belongings before we left town. Again, I was denied a chance to go, but it didn't really matter anymore. The kids were gone.

Mom tried hard to ignore the blood-spattered scene and concentrate on getting the things on my list. She was careful to get the family portrait, which lay on the floor beside the television and my anniversary roses, half-wilted on the kitchen table.

Dad looked for more evidence. He found the place where Greg fell in the yard. Very little blood stained the grass. He must have died quickly.

Inside the house, he found two holes in the front door and one through the bunk beds, as if the killers had just fired haphazardly about the room. The wall beside the spot where Stacy died was splattered three feet up with blood, as if a small explosion occurred. He hoped it meant she died quickly, too.

The floor under the couch was riddled with holes and soaked with blood. A bullet mark in the metal frame of the couch where a shot had ricocheted sent chills up his spine. He imagined Steve under the couch, wounded and unable to move, lying there as the shots kept coming. Billy kept firing, but Steve just wouldn't die.

He pulled back the covers of the master bed, my bed, where Tonya had fled to hide. Blood soaked the mattress clear through. The autopsy indicated that all four of the bullets in Tonya were potentially fatal. But there was too much blood. Tonya didn't die fast. She bled to death. He wept that she might have been saved, if only we could have gotten there quicker.

* * *

George and I sat in the motel room scanning the three newspapers Don had brought with him in the morning. Our story was on the front page of each one.

The Springfield News-Leader read: "Slaying of Children Stuns Area Residents." A picture of two officers investigating evidence inside the house was printed beside a copy of my new family portrait. I had no idea when I got it in the mail that it would be on the front page the next day.

The headline of *The St. Louis Globe-Democrat* read: "Two Questioned in Killing of Four Children." It said that two of George's guns, the .22 pistol and a .357 Magnum that had never been fired, were missing from the house. The murderers had used our own guns to kill the kids.

The Kansas City Times was the most detailed of all. Individual pictures of the children were splashed across the top. I wondered how the reporters got them. The headline read: "Lake Area Baffled by Slaying of Four Children."

Reporters had interviewed a few of our Kansas City neighbors, and their kind words about our family did more good than any sympathy card could.

"They were the most polite kids," Mrs. Terril, a former neighbor was quoted. "The boys were just as nice as they could be. My car got stuck in the snow and the boys came and tried to help. I offered to pay them but they wouldn't take it. You know, the oldest boy I would like to have kept."

"The boys were perfect gentlemen," said another neighbor, Harvey Shepard. "They were the kind of kids who would ask permission to get a ball if it went over the fence into our yard. They were such well-behaved kids."

I smiled at that one, remembering the day Steve came to me to discuss the crush he had on Harvey's daughter. He wanted to know how to go over and properly introduce himself, but he was too shy. Maybe that's why the ball went over the fence. How could this boy's life be over already?

I read the testimonials over and over again. I was so proud that others remembered the fine qualities of my children. They touched so many people. Nobody could say anything bad about our kids.

I sat on the bed all morning staring down at the pictures of the kids in the paper, hugging it tight against my chest and rocking it like I would Baby Stacy. It seemed this was the closest anybody was ever going to let me get to the kids again.

Mom, Dad and Don returned from the house with the items I'd requested, and a few more they thought I might want. They did goof on one thing. I'd asked them to get an orange Western shirt of mine from the closet. Instead, they brought a shirt of Steve's that looked a lot like mine. They felt bad about it, but I told them it was quite all right. I hugged the shirt to me, remembering the first time Steve wore it.

Steve's employer had presented him with box-seat tickets to the Camden County Rodeo, kind of a bonus for a job well done. Steve could have shared the tickets with friends from school. But instead, he wanted to treat the family to a night out. The box-seats meant that while everybody else sat in the bleachers, we'd go in style.

My parents were at their cabin for the weekend, so we asked them to babysit Tonya and Stacy. The rodeo would run way past their bedtime, and Stacy would have been impossible to keep in her seat for so long. At one-and-a-half, she could really get around.

Steve bought himself a new orange Western shirt to wear with his favorite jeans. We were running late the night of the rodeo and Steve was getting worried we wouldn't make it on time. George told me to go ahead and take Steve on to the fairgrounds. He'd run the girls on over to the cabin as soon as Steph was ready and then head that way. He knew the parking would be terrible.

Steve and I had to park blocks away and walk to the arena. As we walked, I slowed to get one pace behind him. I admired his confident gait. He looked really sharp in that orange shirt. I thought how lucky I was to have him for a son. Steve had a special sort of magnetism that just drew people to him.

We cheered the cowboys on through the steer wrestling, bronc riding, and team roping. Stephanie especially liked the women's barrel racing. During half-time, we stomped our feet to the songs of Moe Bandy, who was all dressed up like a rodeo clown.

When it was over we waded through the crowd and made our way back to the pickup. It seemed futile to try to move. We'd just get all tangled up in the traffic. So we all piled into the bed of the truck and looked up at the stars.

We started asking all kinds of philosophical questions about the universe and the meaning of life. An hour passed before Stephanie looked down and announced that we were the only vehicle left in the whole parking lot.

I folded the shirt carefully, preserving the memory of that wonderful night my family shared. There would never be any others to match it.

* * *

We spent part of the day away from the motel, just to get out.

The world outside seemed alien to me. People were concerned and sincere, but hushed. I wondered how they could go about their daily lives after what happened. I thought the whole world should mourn with me.

We went to the barber shop and all got trims for the upcoming funeral services. The barber was quiet, and he wouldn't let us pay for the haircuts. As we walked toward the door to leave, I looked back to nod a thank you. The barber didn't see me. He had turned away. He was crying.

It was several miles from the barber shop to the clinic, where I wanted to refill my birth control pills before we left town. I rode in the back seat, clutching the newspaper that carried pictures of the children, gazing out at scenery I'd passed dozens of times.

I don't think I ever drove all the way to town without at least one of the kids with me, taking Steph to work, or Greg to baseball practice. Never again would they pass this way with me. Excruciating loneliness gripped me from the inside out.

I carried the rolled-up newspaper into the clinic with me. Mom accompanied me, leaving the men in the car. After giving my prescription to the pharmacist, I joined Mom in the waiting area.

Across the room, at the main desk, stood a young mother with a beautiful baby girl about fourteen months old. I watched her intently as the mother passed the baby to a nurse, so her hands would be free to write a check.

"Mom, I want to hold that baby," I said, trembling.

"No, honey, don't. It would only upset the mother."

I watched in silence as the nurse cooed and laughed with the baby. The young mother jabbered away, as if she and the nurse were old friends. I missed Stacy so much. I wanted to touch her, to hug her, to take care of all her little needs.

"Mom, I've got to hold that baby," I whispered.

"No!" Mom insisted, reaching out to grab my hand.

I tried to make the feeling go away, but I needed so much to hold that little baby. I was tired of nobody letting me do what I needed to do. I couldn't stand it any longer. Before Mom could stop me, I jumped up and hurried toward the mother.

She was still joking with the nurse when I broke in and, almost crying, asked, "Please, ma'am, may I hold your baby? I promise I won't hurt her. Just for a minute?"

The mother seemed puzzled at my tears. Her eyes met Mom's to question her.

"This is the mother of the Swift children that were killed Thursday..."

Before Mom could finish the sentence the woman's eyes filled with tears. She took the baby from the nurse and handed her over to me. With the baby securely in my arms, the mother wrapped her arms around me and led me to a chair.

"You hold her just as long as you like," she cried.

I held the baby girl on my lap and gently caressed her fine blonde hair and soft, tender skin. I admired her eyes and pixie features. She was so like Stacy!

The baby was confused by all the commotion, and after only a few minutes she turned with outstretched arms to her mother, who was now crying more than I was.

"I know, sweetheart," I said to the child. "Mommies are very special. You can go back to your mommy if you want."

The mother took her baby and held her tight, so thankful to have her precious child. I thanked her for her kindness and walked over to get my prescription.

When we stepped back into the car I noticed Mom was crying. But I was not. I had done what I needed to do. My heart was satisfied for a little while.

We returned to the motel, where we sat for several hours scanning newspapers, making phone calls, doing anything to keep busy. The television was on constantly to receive news updates.

By now it was late afternoon. I hadn't eaten in two days, and no one else had eaten since Don brought the sweet rolls and coffee early that morning. Dad suggested we go to the Nighthawker for dinner, hoping the atmosphere would relax us and stimulate our appetites.

The waitress led us to a booth in the far corner. I stared blankly at the menu. Nothing appealed to me. I had no desire to eat at all.

"Order something," Dad insisted. "Maybe when it comes you'll feel like eating."

I didn't think so, but I ordered a ham dinner with baked potato and a salad. Dad was pleased.

I looked around the crowded restaurant, wondering where Steph and the police chief had sat when he'd treated her to lunch. I recalled a far-away time when we brought the whole family here with Dale's family of five. We occupied a giant table then. Tonya spilled her milk.

My thoughts were interrupted as a plate of food was set before me. I picked up my fork and tried a bite of potato, then of ham, but my body rejected any attempt to nourish it, and after only five bites I gave up. Mom, Dad, and George weren't doing a whole lot better, and they, too, quickly gave up.

We rose from the table and walked to the door. Dad stopped at the counter to pay for our uneaten meals. The waitress saw our nearly full plates and asked if, perhaps, there was something wrong with the food or the service.

"I'm sure it's all very good, Miss," Dad replied. "But we're the parents and grandparents of the Swift children that were killed and, I'm sorry, but we just can't get the food to go down."

The waitress's eyes filled with tears, and she refused to let Dad pay for the meals. We quietly returned to the motel.

* * *

As the sun sank lower in the sky that Saturday night, memories of the children overwhelmed me. For two days now I had longed to hold them, and the emptiness inside grew more vast and cold. Hopes for this life were dashed forever.

More than anything I needed to know if I would ever see my children again. Was I even "worthy" of being reunited with them again someday? And if I was, how long was I going to have to wait?

Who was God, and where was He when my children were dying? How did He feel about this gross injustice done to my little ones? As my thoughts intensified, my inner self throbbed, ached for answers.

George and Dad slipped into town to get the evening newspapers. I told Mom I was going into my room to sort out my feelings alone.

"Honey, I wish you'd stay in here with me," she said. "I'm worried about you."

"I really need to be alone," I insisted. "I have to talk to God." I quietly retreated into my own room.

The darkness enveloped me as I crossed the room to the farthest corner. I sat on the floor facing the wall and closed my eyes. I concentrated on my inner feelings.

I felt like an empty fifty-five gallon drum, cold and hollow. The real me was a tiny speck inside the drum. This tiny speck was screaming for answers, pleading for understanding, but the words only echoed back in the cold, empty space. The outside world was completely shut out. It refused to help me, refused to release me from this prison of grief.

"God!" the tiny speck screamed. "Please, God! Hear me! I can't live without my kids. They're my whole life. What am I supposed to do with myself? I'm a housewife! I can't survive without them. Don't You see? I'm not strong enough. I'm trying so hard to be strong, God, but I can't be! Please, GOD, help me!"

The tiny voice echoed inside the steel drum, bouncing against the sides, seemingly unheard, unreachable to the outside world.

And then something happened.

A hole was punched in the drum, and a fluid, warm and comforting, began to fill it. The tiny speck basked in the security of the fluid, like a fetus in the womb.

The drum filled, and as it filled, my focus began to change. I realized that the drum was me, and the tiny speck was gone. The room came into focus and became the drum, except it didn't feel like a drum anymore, but rather like a warm, secure womb. For a long time I sat relishing the peaceful calmness. And then an answer came.

"You don't have to lose them," came a low, tender voice. "They are in My hands and I am with you. I will give you My strength to see this through."

Suddenly, it felt like all the kids were sitting on my lap. I caressed the air around me as I imagined touching and holding my precious children. A tiny finger reached up to wipe away a tear. I didn't ever want to leave this corner!

Slowly, peacefully, the children faded away. When I realized they were gone, I turned to search for the voice again. I listened intently to the words it spoke.

"You will be with them again. You have not lost them. You are only separated from them for a little while. It has all been taken care of. The answers you seek I will show you in My Book. It has all been written down for you."

The voice drifted away. I sat in the darkness, waiting for more. None came. Still I stayed to reflect on the things I'd heard and felt inside. There was no doubt in my mind that it all was real. I had not imagined it.

I knew, as I rose from that corner, that God went with me. He would give me the strength for the days to come. I didn't have to fight this battle alone. I crossed the room, took the motel Bible from the desk drawer, and carefully opened its pages.

Chapter 11

The Memorial Service

Sunday morning the men went out early to get the newspapers. Without them, we would have known nothing. The police weren't talking. The headline of the *Kansas City Star* read: "Violence Darkens Soul of Ozarks Town." Indeed it had.

The article said the State Water Patrol had recovered George's guns from the cove in front of Ray Richardson's house. The .357 Magnum was found with a magnet after only an hour's search. The .22 was recovered three hours later using scuba gear. Tests confirmed that the .22 pistol was the murder weapon. There was no indication that the .357 Magnum was ever fired.

The fact that his own gun had been misused to kill the very family it was meant to protect was something George found very difficult to deal with. He'd bought the small .22 pistol in 1966 during his years on the police department, and in the eleven years he'd owned it, it had never been used to hurt anyone.

He'd been so careful to teach the children to respect guns, as his father taught him. That should have been enough to keep them safe. It wasn't the gun's fault the kids were killed. Left alone, that gun would have sat in its box on the freezer door from now until the world ended, and never hurt a soul. No, Billy and Ray killed the kids. Not George's gun.

But it still hurt that his guns were the object of lust that led to the killings, that his guns were more precious than his children's very lives. Such a price they had to pay!

He didn't expect to ever get the guns back. They would be kept as evidence for the trial, and thereafter, just in case one of them demanded a new trial later. George decided that if they ever were returned, he'd have them melted down into smooth steel balls, and then he'd throw them back into the lake where they'd been found. I wished I could do the same to Billy and Ray.

It was easy to hate Billy because we knew him. We could picture him in our minds, and remember his evil eyes and shifty demeanor, though the questions of why kept coming.

But we had no idea what Ray looked like or what kind of man he was. He had to be really horrible to help kill four children. He couldn't possibly have had a grudge against them. He didn't even know their names.

* * *

At noon we packed the car and left the motel for the last time. A memorial service was scheduled for two o'clock at the Lakeland Baptist Church. Pastor Turner was to officiate. Though the children's bodies wouldn't be present, we felt it only right to give the lake people a chance to say good-bye.

We drove in silence to the Big Apple Restaurant a good fifteen miles away. A banquet table was set for us in a private dining room with a big white Sunday table cloth and yellow flowers in the center. Don Turner and his family were already there along with several church members I didn't know. We awkwardly took our places.

I have no idea what I had for lunch. I didn't order much, but it was the first meal since the kids were killed that went down and stayed. I fidgeted with my food, feeling like I was in a place I didn't belong. Others made small talk and tried to get George and me to join in. But we weren't up to much conversation with strangers.

I got up to visit the ladies' room only to find a woman already waiting outside the door. Sounds of children playing drifted out of the restroom.

The woman frowned. "Children really shouldn't be allowed to go to the bathroom unattended," she said.

"Yeah," I smiled. "But kids will be kids."

The woman looked a little embarrassed. "Oh, are those your children in there?"

"No," I shook my head, and turned my gaze to the pattern in the carpet. Just then Mom came up behind me.

"This is the mother of the Swift children who were killed Thursday," she informed the woman.

The woman's face seemed to flush with shame for her remarks about the children in the restroom. She rounded the corner and disappeared.

Just before two, we headed over to the church. The parking lot was packed. Singing voices drifted from the crowded sanctuary as we entered the foyer. We paused there to gather our wits. George wrapped my arm through his own, took a deep breath for courage, and pulled open the big double door.

A hundred eyes met us at once as the congregation turned to stare in sympathy. I looked at all my friends and neighbors, their hearts silently reaching out to me, yet not one spoke a word. They didn't have to. Compassion glimmered in each teary eye.

"Stand up straight," Dad whispered to me. "Pull your shoulders back and walk proud."

I squared my shoulders and started down the aisle. I passed a resort owner whose children had played with the boys, and I could hold back the tears no longer. George pulled me ahead to the first pew. Mom passed me a tissue and kept one for herself.

Flowers of every hue lined the tables on either side of the pulpit, reflecting the love of the people even more. Pastor Turner preached a short message summarizing the tragedy of four lost lives and the sacrifice that Christ made for them. His words were comforting and gave me hope that one day I would see the children again.

Toward the end of the service a man with a rich baritone voice sang a song called, "Safe in the Arms of Jesus." I closed my eyes and listened to the words of promise, imagining my children safe in Jesus' arms with no more worries of pain and terror. "Sweetly their souls would rest."

The words touched George so deeply that, after the service, he asked Don for a copy of the song. Don found an old hymnal and tore the page out of it to give to him.

As I listened to the words, I thought of Stephanie going through the chemotherapy treatments. I wondered how long it would be before her soul would rest with the others. How much pain did she still have to endure? And would she beat the cancer before it beat her? Would we at least get to keep one of our children?

After the service, a bubbly young woman hurried to us, her high heels clattering against the tile floor. She grabbed George and me to get our full attention. Her face radiated peace.

"I lost my thirteen-year-old son to drowning three weeks ago," she said smiling. "And I'm just so happy because now he's with Jesus."

George said something stupid just to be a gentleman, his tongue tripping over his teeth. "I'm happy for you," he blurted. But neither one of us could fathom her words. How could she possibly be happy that her son was dead? Even if our kids were in heaven and safe with Jesus we weren't ready to be happy. Comforted, yes. But the kids were no longer with us. We would never hug them again in this life, never share a happy memory with them, never watch them grow. How could we possibly be happy? The very idea seemed incomprehensible.

* * *

After the memorial service, we met with some of our neighbors downstairs in the fellowship room. Mrs. Larson sat hunched in a corner chair, crushed under the weight of guilt for bringing Billy into our lives.

"I never liked that kid," she said trembling. "I knew he was trouble."

We tried to comfort her. "It's nobody's fault," I said. "You couldn't have known. None of us could."

She looked up from her handkerchief. "He shot up some of my best cooking pans and some of my little grandson's baby toys," she said. "That's why I insisted they move out. He was just so destructive."

She didn't say what he shot them up with, and we were too polite to ask her. None of us knew Billy was capable of this much violence. But we all felt guilty for not seeing the signs that led to the killings. If only we could have known. If only the boys at school had told somebody. Anybody!

Debbie Balentine, barely eighteen years old, meekly came to us and held out her arms like a toddler. George reached out to her, and she fell into his arms. He hugged her tight as her tears spilled out in little sobs.

Debbie was the one who drove into the driveway that night. She was the reason Billy and Ray fled the house before stealing all the guns. She had come to deliver a message that Stephanie could come home for the weekend. She arrived just after eight o'clock, less than an hour after we left to go play Bingo.

When nobody answered her knock, she opened the front door just a little to call out. She could swear she saw movement through the curtains as she pulled in. Her eyes fell on the form of Stacy, her bottle and blanket at her side.

"She had blood all over her," Debbie whimpered, remembering the horrible scene. "But her leg only had a little trickle on it. I went into shock. I thought to myself, 'Stacy's just hurt. Her leg is scratched, but she's all right.'"

She walked over to the baby to examine the scratch, and then spied Steve under the couch, bloody and lifeless. Whirling in fear, she encountered Tonya curled up on the crimson bed.

Stunned by the sight, she began to call out for Greg. When he did not answer, she fled from the house. As she jumped into her car, she heard an engine start next door and realized her own life might be in danger. She pulled out of the driveway and sped toward home, crying hysterically all the way.

Since her parents were away, she went to a neighbor's house to call the police. She told them the children were hurt real bad, or they were dead. Not knowing how to give the exact directions to our house, Debbie had no choice but to go with the officer and lead him to the scene. She waited in the patrol car when he went in. The officer found Greg in the yard.

Debbie knew we were members of the American Legion and that we often played Bingo on Thursday nights. That's how we were located so quickly. How Pete got the job of telling us, I'll never know.

George comforted Debbie as if she were his own daughter, stroking her long dark hair as she trembled in his arms.

"If you ever need somebody to talk to about this," he told her, trying to make his voice sound soothing and fatherly. "If you ever need anything at all, you let us know. It's going to be hard to live with what you saw."

"I know," she cried. "I can't get it out of my mind. It just keeps coming back."

Oh Debbie, I thought to myself, I'd give anything in the world if you hadn't had to walk in on that. I thanked God they didn't kill her too. I could never have lived with the guilt.

We said our good-byes to neighbors and comforted their children. We found ourselves doing a lot of comforting.

Before leaving, Don led us back up to the sanctuary to decide what to do with all the flowers. I wanted to take all of them with us, but it just wasn't feasible. There were too many.

Pastor Turner suggested we donate them to a nursing home to brighten the rooms of the elderly. After studying each one carefully and removing the cards, I finally agreed to let him take all of them with the exception of two large plants.

The first one was a big beautiful fiddle leaf fig tree that stood a good three feet tall. Its leaves, the size of violins, were waxed shiny. The card was signed, "The Camdenton Junior High School."

I could just imagine the junior high students buzzing about the halls, taking up a collection for flowers. Perhaps it was a counselor who suggested a living plant would last longer than a cut bouquet.

I could see two or three teenaged representatives going to the florist with the proceeds to pick out a suitable one. Judging by the size of the huge fig, they'd picked the biggest one available to show their love for the kids. In their own way, they were saying, "We grieve with you." And being from children, it meant more to me than they could ever know.

The second one, a large schefflera that spread like a canopy over its pot, had a long card attached that was personally signed by every player on Greg's Little League team, representing five grades.

To me, every leaf on the schefflera represented a child with a baseball mitt on his hand. Every leaf was a sympathy note of its own. Like pennies from heaven, they filled my heart.

We packed the two plants into the car. The fig sat on the back seat floorboard and bent at the ceiling. The schefflera was crammed into the Volkswagen's hatchback beside the sacks of clothes and bundles of newspapers.

As we said our last good-byes at the church, Stephen and Mary Pyeatt rumbled into the parking lot. Stephen piled out of the Blazer and stuffed a wad of money into George's hand.

"This is from just three days with a collection jar," he said. "You take it. You may need it for expenses."

George stuffed the wad into his slacks and hugged him. I was already at the other side of the car hugging Mary.

"We're going to try to drive down and make it to the funeral," Stephen said. "You call and let us know exactly when it is."

"I'll do that," George promised. "You guys take care. We're going to miss you."

He slapped George on the back in a friendly gesture and climbed back into the Blazer. With tearful good-byes, they pulled away.

* * *

I rode in the back seat beside Mom, slouching as best I could in the compact car, and watched in silence as my Ozark hills passed me by. The scraggly trees, like old friends, waved a sorrowful farewell and I glanced back to see if they turned to watch my passing.

I was leaving my home for good. I was leaving behind all my friends, all the people who banded together and took the time to care. Everything that connected my life with the kids was getting farther and farther away.

We had come to the Ozarks with so many dreams for the future. Now I was leaving my paradise behind, both of us crippled by the brutal slayings. My life would never be the same. And for me, neither would the Ozarks.

Soon the scenery of the Ozarks would be replaced by city streets. For a brief moment I panicked. It made no sense to go back to the big noisy city. I was a part of those hills. They were a part of my children and me. I didn't want to go.

"Joy," George interrupted my thoughts. His eyes gleamed happily. "Look at the ducks." He pointed out the window.

I scrunched down in the seat and peered into the sky. Four mallard ducks flew directly above us.

For as long as I could remember we'd watched for the ducks this time of year. I always felt a sort of fascinated freedom watching them fly in perfect V formation, heading to a new place. If George were driving he'd have pulled over like we always did, so the kids could pile out and watch them.

"Oh, George," I whimpered. "I wish the kids could see them."

I gazed out at the four free spirits flapping to keep close to one another, like children playing follow-the-leader. They weren't flying south as they should. They were flying west with us.

George turned to me with a glint of a smile. "Maybe the kids are the ones who sent them."

I looked up at them and smiled. "Maybe so," I said dreamily.

We watched the quartet for miles, engulfed in our own philosophical thoughts. Maybe the ducks were the kids' way of comforting me, of telling me that no matter where I went they'd continue to be a part of me. I knew in my heart that I would never forget them.

At last the ducks veered south and disappeared.

Chapter 12

Mount Moriah

W hen we stopped at Jean's apartment, Stephanie was lying on the couch with an old quilt around her. She looked so frail, so much weaker than when I'd seen her last. She started crying the minute we walked in the door. George bent down to hug her.

"Dad, I'm the only one left," she choked on the words.

George held her tighter. His bloodshot eyes burned back the tears. "I need you more than ever now, Punkin," his voice crackled. The lump in his throat sounded like another piece of his heart giving way. Such a battered organ, I wondered what kept it pumping.

Jean was drinking from a glass of wine, and it was clear she'd had just a little too much to drink. But her sister had flown in from Chicago, so someone was there to keep things in check. Besides, it was probably helping her deal with the grief. She had done little more than wait for the past three days until we arrived to start the funeral arrangements. She had to do something to make the wait bearable.

I really didn't know how Jean was going to react to me being in her house. That first day at the hospital with Steph had been so tense.

She told Steph once that she never wanted to meet my daughters. Right after Stacy was born, George took Tonya with him to drop the other three off to visit Jean. Jean said she needed to talk to him before he left, and George had no choice but to bring Tonya in with him. Steph told me later that her mother cried after he left.

George was the one I felt sorry for. This was going to be tough enough on him without the two mothers acting like a couple of bobcats. There was no way to separate the two families for the funerals, and I didn't want to. I considered the boys my sons, though I never tried to take Jean's role from her.

I hurt for Jean, and I hurt with her, because I loved her sons as much as I did my daughters. I understood, as no one else could right now, what it felt like to be a mother and lose her children to murder.

Jean must have felt it too because she seemed very concerned about the way I was taking the loss. As long as we remained concerned for each other, we'd get through this thing.

Mom was anxious to get home to her own family, so we didn't stay as long as George would have liked. We made arrangements with Jean to meet at Mount Moriah in the morning and headed across town.

We arrived to mass confusion at the Kirkham apartment. My sister Dawn and twenty-year-old brother Rick, who still lived at home, were there with their steadies, Doug and Cindy. My oldest brother, Jack Jr., had driven up from Rolla with his wife Claudette and their two-year-old son, Jack III.

The kitchen looked like a catering service had come in. There were pies and cakes, casseroles, hams and all kinds of homemade specialties dropped off by friends.

Visitor's names, what they'd left and telephone messages were scribbled furiously on any wadded paper that was at arm's reach at the time. Sympathy cards were already piling high.

I found four postcards George had mailed from the hospital the day before the kids were killed. One was addressed to each of the boys, one to Tonya and Stacy together, and one to me.

On the front of mine was a picture of a dilapidated old building, weathered and time-worn, with "natural air conditioning." On the back George had written, "With a little paint and a lot of love, it just might be home."

I smiled through my tears. Our house was a home, not because of the things we owned, but because of the love we all put into it. It would never be the same without the children. I read the children's cards and grieved that they would never get to see them.

Little Jack toddled about the crowded room, confused by all the emotion around him. Why were Uncle George and Aunt Joy here without the kids? They never came without the kids. Steve always gave him horsey rides on his knee.

"Aunt Joy," my little nephew tugged at my leg. "Where's the kids?"

Claudette knelt beside him and explained that the kids had gone to heaven to be with God, and they were very happy there.

Jack III pondered a minute. Heaven sounded very nice, especially with all the kids there. "Can I go too?" he asked innocently.

Claudette grabbed him up and buried her face in his shoulder.

"No more, God," I thought. "We've lost too many."

* * *

Monday morning we drove down to the burial sites George's mom had selected. They were one row down from George's dad, the closest she was able to get five plots in a row. The lawn sloped gently down toward the cemetery lake, and a big tree grew on the corner of the last plot to shade the graves from the hot summer sun. We were satisfied with the site.

Jean was already waiting when we went inside the funeral home. This whole funeral thing was going to be a delicate balancing act, trying to keep two mothers happy. From the start, the funeral director and his staff treated George and me as the parents, with Jean as secondary. George would have to play the middleman to make sure neither mother was slighted.

After some time in an office giving specific information about the kids and next of kin for announcements, we were led downstairs to a room with eight caskets.

I had originally wanted all four of the caskets to look alike. I hoped Jean would not balk at the idea, wanting her children to be separate from mine. Now here they stood, four caskets exactly alike; two six-foot ones for the boys, a five-foot one for Tonya, and a four-foot one for Stacy.

They were a deep bronze color with a dignified traditional style to them. To me, they seemed rather old for the kids, like something you'd bury an elderly gentleman in.

There were two other six-foot boxes. They were metallic silver, and the style seemed almost...well, almost like a fine Corvette. They seemed to match our half-grown sons' lively spirits and fine tastes. The boys would have approved.

The other two smaller caskets were framed in wood and covered in pink crushed velvet with a raised rosebud pattern. Their curved ends made them resemble a delicate jewelry box, or a china doll's cradle if rockers were added to the bottom. Their linings were white satin and lace, a little girl's delight.

Jean studied the silver caskets carefully, then turned to the funeral director behind her. "Can we get an orange lining for Greg's?" she asked.

The funeral director shuffled his feet. "I'm afraid there isn't time before the service."

Jean looked at George like a begging puppy. Anyone who knew Greg wouldn't think this was such a strange request. Practically everything the boy owned had orange in it. Three-fourths of his shirts were orange. He loved oranges and orange juice. And all of the woodworking projects we built together were painted orange. It was no surprise that his favorite animal was the tiger.

Still, an orange lining might have been too loud and not appropriate for Greg's casket.

"Jean," I suggested. "We could get him an orange pillow. And we could get Steve a blue one."

"Can we do that, George?" Jean asked. All day she seemed so far away, so lost in the clouds.

"You bet," he said, happy to resolve the orange issue quickly. George stood back and let Jean and me choose the flower sprays to decorate the caskets. Since we had gotten into colors with the pillows, it was decided that the sprays would be in blue and orange for the boys to individualize them. The girls' would be matching pink ones to go with their pink velvet caskets. And baby's breath. I wanted lots and lots of baby's breath for all of them.

The next decision was clothing. We wanted Greg buried in the new orange and gray jersey and blue jeans Steph had sent him for his birthday only a few weeks before. But Jean insisted they'd have to be washed to soften them. She refused to bury him in new stiff jeans.

Steve would wear his favorite rodeo shirt, but we'd have to buy him a pair of jeans to go with it. The girls would need dresses, and all of them would need socks and underwear.

George's mom agreed to go to Sears and get clothes for the kids. She also bought two yards of cotton material in bright orange and bold blue, and took them home to Aunt Georgie's to make the pillowcases for the boys.

Since Mount Moriah had its own large chapel, we decided to have the funeral service here to avoid the long highway procession to the burial site. We expected a lot of guests.

By late afternoon all the arrangements were made. Jean left for home to be with Steph. George and I returned to my parents' apartment with plans to return to the funeral home in the morning.

The evening newspaper announced that Ray Richardson had been arraigned at two o'clock that afternoon. He was charged with four counts of capital murder and was ordered held without bond pending trial.

The juvenile (we knew it was Billy Dyer) was being charged with juvenile delinquency in the murders. He would undergo psychological testing to determine whether he should be tried as an adult. I prayed with all my might that he would. Given the chance, I would have killed them both with my bare hands.

Deputy Sheriff Skipper Hedges told reporters that they had a motive for the killings, but he refused to divulge it, saying, "Once you know what it (the motive) is, if you ever know, if it eventually comes out in court, you'll know why we can't say anything."

His statement puzzled us.

* * *

When we got to the funeral home Tuesday morning the kids had been dressed, placed in their caskets and taken to the chapel ready for the service the following day. George and I were escorted into the chapel by a young man in a light blue suit. Flowers surrounded the caskets on three sides.

The caskets had been placed side by side, Tonya and Stacy in the middle, flanked by Greg and Steve. I was satisfied with the placement. It only seemed natural to have the boys protecting their baby sisters.

I had openly expressed my need to see the kids; not to see the wounds, but to accept that the children really were dead and to say good-bye. But Dad told me to remember them the way they were. He couldn't imagine how the mortician could possibly patch up the holes and repair the girls' open scalps. I promised him I wouldn't ask to see them.

For six days now I had tried to be where the children were; in the house, at the morgue and now here at the funeral home. I remembered what Dad had said, but I needed so much to open the caskets and touch the children one last time. How could I know these really were my kids in these boxes? Maybe they weren't dead at all. Maybe they were still out there somewhere, alive.

George and I drifted from casket to casket, laying our hands on the smooth metallic and soft velvety surfaces, speaking softly to each individual child. I felt like a child myself, being allowed to be here, but not to touch or to look for fear I would spoil something. I was so tired of others being in charge, forbidding me to do what I felt I needed to do.

We waded through the sea of delicate, brightly colored flowers, taking the time to read each card that would reveal the giver. On a small pedestal table just behind the caskets sat a slender milk-white vase filled with a dozen long white roses. I drew closer to it and reached for the card. I recognized the handwriting immediately, so polished and perfect. The card read simply, "To my brothers and sisters. Love, Stephanie." I wept for her loneliness.

We left the chapel, intending to return later. Jean came to see the boys while we were gone and demanded they be put next to each other.

That evening we returned to the funeral home to find the caskets had been moved. The kids were now lined up by order of age across the front.

"This won't do," I complained. "Steve is too far away from Stacy. She needs to be closer to him."

The poor funeral director sighed. "We'll change it after you go," he promised.

By now it was getting dark outside. Tomorrow would be the last day we could get this close to the kids, so we lingered just to be near them. I fought with my promise to Dad and my intense need to touch the children just one last time. If they were buried without my touching them, I would never be at peace.

I turned to the funeral director. "I want to see them," I said. "Do you think it would be wise? Will I be sorry if I look at them?"

"They really don't look bad," he said. "You have to do what's in your heart. Don't let anybody tell you what to do because after tomorrow it will be too late."

That was all the encouragement I needed. "I want to see them," I said. "But first we have to get bonnets for the girls. Dad said if I insisted on seeing them, the girls must have bonnets."

"We can push their heads deeper in the pillows," the director offered.

"No, I want to get bonnets. We'll be right back."

We went to three stores in search of summer bonnets to cover our little girls' heads. The stores offered a wide array of stocking caps. But since it was already late September, they had no summer bonnets in stock. It was now after nine, and all the stores were closing.

Defeated, we returned to Mount Moriah to tell the funeral director we'd be back in the morning with bonnets so we could see the kids. We drove in silence back to my parents' house.

* * *

Among the letters we received in the mail that day was a card from the Tidgrens at the Flame Resort where Steve worked.

The card read, "In loving memory of Steve, we are establishing the Steven T. Swift memorial fund with which a long lasting piece of educational equipment will be presented in his name to his biology classroom at school...Carl, Jan and JoBeth Tidgren."

Steve's favorite subject was biology.

The other letter was from Steve's science teacher. I will cherish this letter to my dying day. His letter in part follows:

Dear George and Joy,

As Steve's teacher, I found your son to be an extremely polite, friendly, cooperative student whose personality was one which I fell in love with. For the past five days I've been unable to understand why anyone would have done this to him and the rest of your children. Steve was so very popular and got along with everyone.

When he came into my class he added so much personality and friendliness to it. Personally, I considered Steve to be one of my special students, or favorites. The entire school mourns the loss of two fine junior high boys. I just hope that telling you how I felt about Steve will help you. I've cried my eyes out for almost a week now.

I drove down to the memorial service to pay my last respects. I wanted to sit down and talk with you, but I felt that you were not up to it. If you are ever in Columbia, call me and we'll get together and help each other overcome this tragedy.

Bob Brown.

So many people loved Steve. I was not just a prejudiced parent. Steve was truly special. I lay in bed that night thinking how cold Stacy must be so far away from Steve. I cried softly.

George reached for me in the darkness and pulled me close. I cuddled up next to him, comforted by the touch of his skin against mine. He caressed me tenderly.

"Honey, I love you so much," he whispered. "But I'm so afraid."

"Afraid of what?" I cried.

"Afraid to be intimate," he said. "Afraid it might be somehow sacrilegious after losing the kids. But I need to know that one thing in my life hasn't changed."

"Oh George, I'll always love you. That will never change."

We wept together entwined as one. The gentle caresses grew hungrier and more urgent as we explored each other as if for the first time. Empty aching limbs longed to be assured we weren't alone. Our lovemaking fulfilled our famished bodies, bringing feeling back into our grief-numbed hearts. Giving us strength for the days to come.

Chapter 13

Standing Room Only

W e rose early Wednesday morning and set out in search of bonnets for the girls. We finally found a couple of bright cotton print ones on clearance and quickly snatched them up. They wouldn't match the dresses George's mom had bought for the girls to be buried in; it didn't seem to matter.

We hurried back to Mount Moriah and handed the bonnets over to the funeral director, who placed them on the girls.

"I want roses," I said. "I'd like to give each of the kids a long-stemmed red rose to be buried with them, as a symbol of a promise that we'll love each other forever. Can I do that?"

"You certainly may," the funeral director said. "I'll have the florist downstairs send them up." The flowers arrived, and the funeral director escorted us into chapel.

The acrid smell of formaldehyde was the first thing I noticed as I entered the chapel. As I drew closer to the caskets, the fragrance of a multitude of flowers, twice as many as yesterday, worked to mask the pungent odor of death.

The problem of how to place the caskets had been neatly solved. I had to smile at the funeral director's ingenuity. Steve and Greg were put on higher stands head to foot, with Tonya and Stacy on lower stands in front of them. Now Steve was beside Stacy, and Tonya was beside Greg. But the boys were together and the girls were together, and both Jean and I would be content.

I braced myself for the worst and moved ahead, almost afraid of what I'd see. And then the faces of the children came into view, and the anxiety I had carried for days melted away, as my broken heart reached out for my children. They were mine, all right. It really was them. My God, it was them. Look what they did to my babies. Why, Billy? Why did you do it? What had we done?

I couldn't help but marvel at the mortician's skill. No open wounds were visible, no cuts, no stitches. That seemed quite amazing considering the number of bullets that had been pumped into them. Not to mention the autopsies that followed their deaths to retrieve the slugs and determine just which ones actually caused the dying.

Greg actually looked peaceful. Not the least bit of worry showed on his brow. He did need a haircut. His coarse brown-blonde hair lay across his forehead and curled at the ends.

The fine satin lining of his casket seemed a bit too fancy for this perpetually dirty happy-go-lucky boy. But the orange pillow that cradled his head matched his character perfectly.

His fingers were cut and scarred from twelve years of rough-and-tumble play. I slipped a rose under his hands, which were neatly crossed at his waist.

"This is for you, Greg, " I whispered. "It is our promise that we'll love each other and be a family forever. And not even death can take that away from us."

If I could just somehow ignore the silver metallic casket, I could imagine that my adventurous fun-loving son was just sleeping, dreaming happily of frogs and snails, and goin' fishing. It seemed a shame to wake him from his dreams.

But a look of terror could not be erased from the faces of the other three. They had been aware of the horror, the turmoil, the pain. And not even the mortician's skillful hands could wipe it away.

I gazed down at Steve, trying to imagine what he'd gone through those last horrible moments before death. His mouth was closed, but his jaw was locked open as if he'd died crying out for mercy.

I looked more closely. He seemed to breathe! I laid my hand on his chest, but it felt like a solid block. It wouldn't rise or fall.

"I'm so proud of you, Steve," I whispered. "You didn't let me down. Don't ever think I was disappointed in you. I told you to watch the girls and I know you did your best."

I placed a rose in Steve's hands, and repeated the love promise I had made to Greg.

George pushed the hair off of Steve's forehead and brushed it to the side. "You became a man that night, Steven," he cried in despair. "I don't know how I'm going to get along without you."

George was right. He had died a man at fourteen, his body never reaching its full height or stature. God, how I wanted Steve to open his eyes and tell his father the nightmare was over. I leaned against the casket and wept, my tears streaming down the sides of the silver-colored coffin.

George took my arm and guided me toward the pink velvet caskets that cradled our daughters. Tonya's little cheeks were all puffed out, her chin held tight against her chest, her eyes squinted shut to block out the horrible pain. The lacy cuffs of her starched navy blue dress seemed too tight on her chubby arms, and the bonnet strings left creases under her neck and hid her fine shoulder-length ash-blonde hair.

I wanted to pick her up and rock her, and take away the terror. Guilt overwhelmed me for leaving her to endure such a nightmare alone. She hid in my bed; she should have been safe there. She must have cried out for me.

Why did they stab such a sweet little girl? What did she do to deserve such a death? She was still so small, yet she was growing up so fast; a little piece of clay just starting to take shape. I'd had such plans for her fourth birthday, now only six days away. But now, any plans we'd made for her future were dashed forever.

Baby Stacy only half-filled her casket. Her cheeks were all purplish and blue, and they looked like they'd been stuffed with tissue. Her face was so misshapen, she didn't even look like herself. But they had managed to completely cover the holes made by the bullet that entered her neck and ripped through her cheek.

The white ruffled panties she wore seemed out of place. My mind told me that Stacy needed a diaper. And where was the bottle and blue satin blanket she carried with her everywhere she went? She wasn't Stacy without them.

"My sweet precious Baby Stacy," I cried. "How could anyone shoot a baby? She couldn't have told. They could have left her."

I stood back and scanned their still young forms. For days I'd wondered what I could have done to prevent their deaths, what I might have done had I walked in on the killings. What Steve might have done if he'd been better prepared. It all happened so fast.

By the looks on their faces, this room should have been filled with cries for help, and screams of terror. Instead there was only silence. Deathly silence. And it made me want to scream, to equalize the tension. To match the senses of sight with sound. But I don't think the funeral director would have appreciated such an outburst.

* * *

We were taken to an office to relax before the funeral, which was to begin at three o'clock. We decided to cancel the limousine and just stay here with the kids all day.

Dad came up later to apologize for trying to talk me out of seeing the kids. "I'm sorry," he said. "I just didn't realize. Would it offend you and George? I just gotta see them too."

"You have to do what's in your heart," I echoed the funeral director's advice.

Dad was escorted in to be with the kids. He returned a half hour later, visibly shaken by the experience.

"I'm sorry, George, Joy," he wept. "I hope you don't get mad at me, but Tonya got to me one last time."

"What do you mean, Dad?" I asked.

"I had chewing gum in my pocket," he shuttered back the tears. "I couldn't resist her. I put the whole pack of gum in her hand beside the rose."

He could barely finish before the dam broke behind his eyes and gushed forth in a torrent of sobs.

Tonya and Pa had become best buddies that summer. Dad always carried chewing gum in his pocket, and whenever Tonya saw him, she'd climb into his lap and say, "Pa, you got any gum?" He was never able to resist those big brown eyes. Tonya was his sunshine, and now that she was gone, his world seemed terribly dark.

Dad eventually gained his composure enough to go in and see the kids a few minutes longer before returning home to bring the family to the funeral.

Two guest books were set at the door for people to sign; one for George and me, and one for Jean. So many people came to the funeral that they had to open up the two sets of double doors in the back and set up chairs in the overflow room.

George and I were kept in an office until all the guests arrived. We entered the family seating area to find it filled beyond capacity. Stephen and Mary Pyeatt stood against the back wall with a classmate of Steve's. We were told the young lady had a terrible crush on Steve and was taking his death very badly. Pastor Turner was there, too.

We dodged the maze of metal folding chairs and made our way to the first pew in front of the window overlooking the chapel. From this angle we couldn't really see the guests in the big room, only the caskets up front.

Stephanie sat in a wheelchair beside her mother. Jean's sister and Paula, a friend who flew in from California, sat to the left of them. Seeing us coming, Paula stood up.

"Here, George," she insisted. "You sit by Jean. She needs you to be with her right now."

A space was quickly made for George to slide in between Stephanie and Jean. I meekly took a place on the other side of Stephanie. George wrapped his arm around Stephanie and rested his hand on my shoulder. He rolled his eyes and winked at me to let me know that, though he was doing what duty forced him to do, his heart was with me. I passed him an assuring glance. I had his comfort all the time. Jean only had him this hour.

The drone of whispers hushed when Father Harry Firth stood to speak. George had asked him to perform the service. He had been assigned to the church George and Jean attended back when the kids were very small, and even after he was transferred to a church clear across town, George had sought his counsel.

I don't remember a thing Father Firth said at the service. My mind was years away, recalling those special times I'd shared with my children. The scenes clicked through my memory like an old eight-millimeter projector with no sound. Only close-ups of happy faces, happy moments, moments of laughter and love.

Neither Father Firth nor Pastor Turner had wanted to eulogize the children, perhaps because they were all too young to possess any unique virtues worth mentioning. But as I thought about all those people sitting out there, I wished I could come up with some way to relay to them what wonderful, beautiful children they were, and how very happy we'd been as a family.

Mourners were sent out to their cars for the procession down to the burial site. George and I, and a handful of relatives, were given a few last moments to see the kids before the caskets were sealed.

Jean refused to see them, and convinced Stephanie she shouldn't either. She never even saw the orange and blue pillows she wanted so badly.

I insisted George and I be last in line to see the kids before the caskets were closed. I think I could have stood there forever, not willing to let them be sealed and out of my reach. I wanted the clock to just stop ticking until I was ready to finally say good-bye.

"We have to go," the funeral director urged me on. "I'm sorry."

I bent down to kiss Stacy, but her lips were so cold I couldn't bring myself to kiss the other three. I would just have to be satisfied with the memory of their warm kisses.

We made our way to the limousine as the six pallbearers, all ex-police officers except for Dale, carried the children to waiting hearses. Dale, built like a gorilla, said carrying Stacy's casket was the hardest thing he'd ever had to do. It was so light.

A green tarp, held up by aluminum poles, hung above a single hole sixteen feet wide. The children were placed on the four lowering stands to be buried by order of age, with Stacy closest to a shade tree. Having the girls on the end would allow the tree more room for its roots, since their caskets were shorter than the boys'. Rain began to fall in fine droplets, as if the angels were crying with us.

The graveside service was short, and the people soon gathered back at the funeral home where a visiting room was reserved for our use. To keep curiosity seekers away, we had foregone the visitation the night before. Police officers, friends of George's, were stationed about in plain clothes to ward off any troublemakers. There were none.

George saw old friends and acquaintances he hadn't seen in years, and I awkwardly walked along beside him to exchange pleasantries. Stephanie sat in a wheelchair while old people she didn't know encouraged her to hang in there. Finally the limousine took her and Jean home, and soon afterward the crowd began to filter away.

George and I leaned against the rail of the covered porch and watched as the last of the cars pulled out of the parking lot. Rain fell like a refreshing mist and we reached beyond the rail to catch the fine droplets on our faces and arms.

We felt oddly at peace right now, all alone in the quiet world. The last decisions we would ever make for these four kids, other than picking out flowers, were over forever.

I found it hard to walk away from this place. Most of the relatives on both sides of our family were buried here. It was even comforting to know that someday I would take my place here, in one of the plots bought in 1948 when George's dad was laid to rest. But I never expected to have to bury my children here. I always counted on them having to bury me.

* * *

The day after the funeral, George went alone to talk with Father Firth. Ever since the night at the police station, something had been eating at him. Something Pastor Turner had said: "You should get down on your knees and beg forgiveness for the murderers, for they will feel the wrath of God." Don insisted we were wrong to be so angry, and even insisted on my having a tranquilizer to bring my anger down.

George was trying hard to keep his anger inside for fear that Don was right. But at times it raged so strong he found it hard to control. He told Father Firth about the vengeance he carried. Revenge was his only recourse, yet today's judicial system left no room for such things.

Besides, Billy and Ray were being kept in protective custody to prevent any vigilante actions. George let an officer friend know of his whereabouts at all times, just in case somebody succeeded at getting into the jail and killing them. He knew better than to take the law into his own hands. He wasn't going to commit a crime to punish a crime. He respected the law too much to do that. But he would have cheered if someone else had.

"You have every right to be angry," Father Firth said. "In fact, I'd be more worried about you if you weren't angry."

Father Firth had lost a daughter himself in an accident, and well understood the emotions a father goes through, Christian as well as human.

"To pretend the anger isn't there will only eat holes in you," Father Firth advised him. "You've got to learn to channel the anger. I know you want vengeance, but, 'Vengeance is Mine, saith the Lord. I will repay.' Give it to God and let Him handle it."

"Okay, that's comforting," George thought. At least God understood his need for revenge.

George couldn't think of anything worse than the crime Billy and Ray committed against his children. They deserved to be punished for what they did. He wouldn't apologize for his feelings. He wanted them punished twice; first by the criminal justice system, and then by God later on. No amount of punishment less than death was enough to satisfy his vengeance.

They would indeed feel the wrath of God. But he saw no reason to feel sorry for them. They would be receiving their just desserts for their horrible deed.

And he couldn't forgive them either. How could anybody even expect him to? They had destroyed his family, his life, everything he held dear; his very foundation for existence. To forgive would mean to shrug it off. "Aw, gee, fellas, that's all right. You can kill anything of mine you want. I don't mind."

But he did mind, and he wanted justice.

* * *

I was dealing with more maternal feelings. Though I was still angry, I had vented the worst of my anger early on against the police, and anyone else who threatened to alter my life that night.

I missed being able to take care of the children. I felt so worthless and unnecessary without all the little daily chores that come with motherhood. The kids had been such a huge part of me, such a big chunk of what I really was.

Though neither of us had ever smoked a full pack of cigarettes a day, George and I both were smoking too heavily. Our appetites hadn't fully returned either and I had lost so much weight my cheekbones were showing. I didn't care about myself because I was nothing without the kids. I realized I was very near the brink of self-destruction.

I called Dr. Robert Horseman, the obstetrician who delivered Tonya and Stacy, and asked if I could get an appointment that afternoon. I hoped the doctor would prescribe some vitamins. But more than anything I just needed to talk to somebody who might understand.

Dr. Horseman was a big gentle man with a balding head, a Charlie Chaplin mustache, and a belly the size of a medicine ball. He sang opera when the babies were being delivered to ease the labor pains.

Surely he had to deal with grieving mothers before: mothers of miscarriages, or still births, or sudden infant death syndrome. Perhaps a visit and a checkup would do me some good, both physically and mentally. Like George's visit with Father Firth had done for him.

Dr. Horseman told me to come in at half past four. He'd be done with all his patients by then and could give me the time I needed. He didn't think I needed to see any pregnant mothers in the waiting room right now, either. His nurse showed me to an examining room and took my vital signs. I was fine while we made small talk, but when Dr. Horseman opened the door all the pain and anguish rushed out at once.

Without a word, Dr. Horseman took me by the hand and sat me on his lap like a child. I buried my face in his white coat and acted like one.

"You do understand, don't you?" my heart cried out to him. "You knew how precious my tiny little girls were from the moment they were born. You even commented how beautiful they were at birth. You remember the time I brought my stepsons on a prenatal visit just so I could show them off to you. They were my life! How could they be gone?"

"Let it out, Little One," Dr. Horseman soothed. "Just let it all out." I cried until I couldn't cry anymore.

Dr. Horseman left the room while the nurse assisted me into a gown. He returned a few minutes later to give me a complete checkup. I then dressed and met him in his office.

"Cut down on the cigarettes as much as you can," he said. "Try to eat sensibly, even if you don't feel hungry. And if you ever need someone to talk to, I'm here for you anytime."

I left his office feeling much better. Little did I know that this checkup would mark the beginning of another nightmare.

Chapter 14

Stephanie's Last Days

For Stephanie, the loss of her brothers and sisters gave the cancer the upper hand it needed to win. She just wasn't strong enough to fight the grief and the disease at the same time. She, like the rest of us, found little incentive left in surviving. But for Stephanie, death was a viable option.

Stephanie was taken back to the hospital in Columbia two days after the funeral. We planned to drive down there the next day and stay in a motel for a while. We weren't yet ready to make any long-term plans about a house or a job; not until we knew what Stephanie was going to do. She was our only reason left to hang on.

The radiation machine was down her first two days back, so she missed her treatments. Fluid collected in her abdomen which caused her stomach to swell grotesquely. The rest of her body was a mere skeleton.

Jean came on the weekends, and the three of us took turns sitting with Stephanie. We quit renting the television. Steph's eyes were too strained to watch it. She didn't even read anymore, and preferred to keep the room semi-dark, the curtains drawn.

She just lay there now, sleeping when the pain injections were working, and tossing uncomfortably when they wore off. The tumor against her spine caused her enormous agony. A tube ran out of her side to drain fluid, and a catheter drained her bladder. She adjusted the electric bed constantly to find a comfortable position and begged hourly for something to kill the pain.

No matter what the doctors did, the cancer always seemed three steps ahead of the treatments. I sat beside her bed and watched as her life drained out of her, helpless to stop the flow. We looked for small victories, tiny improvements in her condition to raise our spirits and give us hope. But we waited longer for each one, and at times the waiting was unbearable.

On September 27, six days after the funeral, we returned to Mount Moriah to remember Tonya's fourth birthday. We placed a dozen yellow and white daisies on her unmarked grave, and cried that she hadn't lived to see the presents Grandma had already bought for her. We decided then that Tonya's color would always be yellow, to match her pixie blonde hair.

We fed the ducks from what was left of a bag of potato chips for Tonya, and headed back to Columbia to be with Stephanie.

We learned that Billy Dyer had been transferred to the Missouri Mental Health Building for his psychological evaluation. We walked by that building every day on our way to the front door of the hospital. I hated that he was so close to our last surviving child. I both feared for her life, and wished I had the courage to walk over there and end Billy's. I still fought with the vengeance I carried, and wondered about this boy I had taken so much time to care about. How could I still care after what he'd done?

I spent many hours in the hallway outside Steph's room with a Bible in my hand, trying to learn more about this God who was now responsible for my children's welfare. I made the mistake of starting on page one and found the wars and killings of the Old Testament appalling. I got almost no comfort out of it, and very few answers to my many questions.

I asked for a minister to come to the hospital chapel to talk with me. I needed to know why God was letting all this happen to my family. Why my innocent children were being forced to endure such agony and death. How did God feel about what was happening, and did He will all of this to happen? Were George and I being punished for something we did?

The young Presbyterian minister sat stunned as I explained the details of the events of the last few weeks. When the questions came, he couldn't give me a single answer.

"Well?" I asked when I had talked myself dry.

"Mrs. Swift," he shook his head. "I don't know what to say. I can't think of one thing to say to comfort you. I'm sorry." He left me in the back pew and walked out the door.

I sat there in a daze. This was supposed to be a man of God! He went to college and studied the Bible. So why couldn't he give me the Biblical answers as to why I was going through all this pain and loss? There had to be answers. God promised me it was all taken care of. He told me it was all written down in His Book. So why couldn't the minister point it out to me? I determined to search it out on my own.

* * *

Stephanie grew weaker each and every day. She was hooked up to a heart monitor and one of us was with her constantly. I sat beside her bed in the padded chair, picking at my nails with a pen knife, taking my turn at the watch. The room was morbid without the sunlight. The only sound came from the heart monitor blipping its assurance that she was still alive.

On October 4, George and I arrived at the hospital to find Stephanie screaming in the hallway. We dashed down the hall to see what was the matter. Stephanie lay on a gurney ready to be wheeled down to chemotherapy. Two male aides struggled to keep her down. Steph saw us coming. Her face was filled with fear.

"Dad, don't make me go!" She clung to Harry T. Hound. "It hurts too bad. I don't want to go!"

"Stephanie," one of the aides scolded. "You have to go."

"No," she pleaded again. "Just today, don't make me go. I'm tired. It hurts too much. Please, Daddy! Please, tell them not to make me go!"

Her appeal for mercy tore at our already shredded hearts. It wasn't going to matter if she missed just one day. She would live or she would die. Today wasn't going to change a thing.

"Take her back," George demanded. "She doesn't have to go today."

The aides shrugged and wheeled her back into her room. I dashed away to the elevator to prevent Stephanie from seeing my turmoil, and went straight to the chapel downstairs. I walked boldly up to the alter and stood before it. I didn't want to be in that back pew where the minister had insisted we sit. I wanted to be face to face with God.

"GOD! Don't let her hurt anymore!" I demanded, my fists clenched, my teeth grinding in outrage." 'She's been through enough. You heal her now, God. And if You can't heal her now, then You take her now. She can't take any more pain!"

I collapsed into the front pew and buried my face in my hands. "Please, God," I cried. "Have mercy on Stephanie. For Steph's sake, not mine."

I sat in the pew for a long time, hoping God would talk to me, would give me some comfort. Nothing came. I finally gained my composure enough to go back upstairs.

George and I stayed the rest of the afternoon taking turns beside Stephanie. She slept most of the time, curled up like an infant, seemingly content in her dreams. I desperately wanted to get a snack and something to drink. But whenever I rose to leave, she'd waken and ask where I was going, and I'd return to my post to endure the hours. I watched the heart monitor blip grow weaker.

We returned to the motel earlier than usual to get some rest. I was exhausted. We shed our clothes and lay on the bed together to watch a movie.

At nine o'clock George felt an urgent need to be with Stephanie. He threw on his dirty clothes and kissed me good-bye. "You stay here and rest," he said. "I won't be long."

At the hospital he found Stephanie sleeping soundly, her eyelids not fully closed, as if it took too much effort to shut them all the way. He sat beside her bed for an hour or more. She never stirred.

He finally decided to go on back to the motel. He kissed her on the forehead and caressed her cheek.

"Stephanie, I love you," he said softly.

She opened her eyes weakly and peered up at him.

"I love you too, Dad."

She closed her eyes again, and drifted back into the secret land he could not enter. George left with a peaceful feeling that everything was going to be all right.

* * *

George had already showered and was half-dressed when I woke up the next morning at seven o'clock.

"Why didn't you wake me?" I asked, pulling the covers away to get up.

The Swift family 1976. Left to right: Greg, Grandma Swift, Joy holding Stacy, Tonya (in front), George, Stephanie, Steve.

Top left:
Stephanie Jean Swift, age 16.

Top right:
Tonya, age 3. Photo taken two
weeks before murders.

Middle:
Greg, age 12.

Bottom:
Steve, age 14.

Stacy, 17 months, with mom, Joy Swift. Photo taken September 1977, two weeks before murders.

Stephanie meets Tonya for the first time, November 1973.

George Swift, 1977, the day the Swifts moved into their new house.

Steve's new Yamaha 100. Friend Jobeth Tidgren looks on.

(Kansas City Star)

Top:
The empty Swift house the
day after the children were
murdered.

Opposite:
Billy Dyer at his arraignment.
At 14, he was being held as a
juvenile, but later charged as
an adult for the brutal crime.

Billy Dyer in his cell at the Missouri State Penitentiary, March 1988.

Mt. Moriah Cemetery, where the kids fed ducks and skipped rocks.

The Swift family, October 1986. Joy, Matt (6), Michael (4), Sandy (8), George.

Joy and George Swift. October 1993.

The Swift children today. Matt, 13, Michael, 11, and Sandy, 15.

He kissed me tenderly. "You lay back down and get some rest. I'll be back to get you at nine thirty."

"Okay," I said, pulling the covers back over me. "But don't forget me."

"I'll be back." He winked and walked out the door.

At 8:45, there was a knock at the door. I answered it to find the motel clerk standing outside.

"Your husband called," she said. "He wants you to take a cab to the hospital right away."

"What's the matter?" I asked. "Did he say what was wrong?"

"No, he just said to come quickly," she answered. "If you like, I'll go down and call you a taxi."

I rushed about the room frantically gathering my clothes. My shoelace knotted up, and I cursed it in disgust. I grabbed the shoe and hobbled down to the lobby, but the cab hadn't yet arrived. I sat nervously working on my shoelace, aware of every second that passed.

"Hurry," my mind kept pushing. "You must hurry."

I freed the knot and slipped my shoe on just as an old cab drove up.

"To the hospital, please!" I said, as I slid into the back seat and slammed the door.

When we arrived at the hospital I leaped from the car and rushed for the elevator. It seemed far slower than it had the hundred odd other times I'd ridden it. When the elevator opened on the third floor, George and Jean stepped into it.

"It's over, Honey," George murmured. "She's gone."

"No!" I cried, dazed by the suddenness of it. "I didn't get to say good-bye!"

George's voice quavered. "None of us did, Punkin."

My legs felt like rubber. I had so wanted to be there in those last moments. I wanted to comfort her, to ease her passing. Why had I slept this morning?

We spent the next hour signing papers and making arrangements for transport to Mount Moriah. We decided to have an autopsy done to help the doctors determine exactly what killed her. When they'd diagnosed the cancer, they said they couldn't tell if it had started recently, or many years before. Without an autopsy they would never know the full extent of the disease. Perhaps what they learned might help the next child, and save another parent from the grief we were experiencing now.

Jean wanted to donate her organs, but they were too riddled with cancer for any use. We would have donated all the kids' organs if they'd been savable. All their deaths were so in vain. Not one good thing came out of them.

Stephanie's things were packed into Jean's car for the long trip back to Kansas City. We waited till a friend arrived by bus to drive her car home for her. She was in no condition to drive. The box of names for Stephanie's Lamb was never opened. It would forever remain the Unnamed Lamb.

I looked back at the Columbia Hospital a final time before stepping into the car. Our last child, the one we'd clung to, was now dead, a mere twenty days after the murder of our healthy four. No court in the world would convict Billy and Ray of murdering Stephanie. But their actions against the others caused her to deteriorate more rapidly.

Would Stephanie have lived longer than seven weeks if she'd stayed home and never had the surgery? Would the chemotherapy have beaten the cancer if her body didn't have the extra burden of her grief? These are questions that will never be answered. I don't have the medical knowledge to form an intelligent hypothesis. But I doubt that she'd have gone any quicker.

* * *

We arrived back at Mom and Dad's apartment late in the afternoon. Mom was still at work, but Dad was there. He'd just lost his job because his boss couldn't handle all the grief our family represented. On top of all the added expenses of helping us and trying to hold everything together, they'd taken away his means of support. Everything seemed so unfair.

A stack of mail awaited us. More sympathy cards. Another church was putting us on their prayer list. And a letter from Dr. Horseman. I tore the envelope open and began to read.

""We regret to inform you that your pap smear has tested positive for cancer cells. Please call the office..."

I threw the letter down angrily and stomped across the room.

"That's it, George!" I ranted. "You're the last of the Swifts now. I might as well just jump out a window and end it all. I'm not going through what Steph just went through. I'm not doing it."

George recovered the letter from the floor. There was that word again...cancer. His face went blank.

Dad grabbed the letter out of his hands and read it for himself. I paced the floor angrily, ready to tear something apart if it got in my way. Wasn't Satan satisfied yet? Hadn't he taken enough?

"Joy, calm down," Dad reasoned. "Call your doctor, and let's find out what's going on."

I paced away enough anger to dial the number. As soon as Dr. Horseman answered, I started in on him.

"What is this," I demanded. "The final kick in the teeth?"

It didn't register. "What do you mean?" the doctor asked.

"The day my last child dies of cancer, and the first thing I read when I get home says that I've got cancer, too?"

"Calm down, Little One," he soothed. "The test showed a very faint positive. It may be nothing at all. I'd like to put you in the hospital for a couple of days, do a biopsy and conization, and if it's cancer, chances are we can take care of it then."

"Okay," I answered, calmed a bit but still sarcastic. "So, when do you want me? I'll be there in the morning if you say so."

Dad called from the living room. "No, honey. If it can wait, let's get past the funeral."

The funeral would be Friday. I was to check into the hospital the following Tuesday.

We met Jean at Mount Moriah the next morning. By now we were seasoned pros at funeral arrangements. This time we were taken into a room filled with caskets. George held me back to let Jean choose. But the selection overwhelmed her.

She eyed a fine white casket with gold trim. Surprisingly, she asked me what I thought of it.

"It's beautiful," I commented. "It looks like it's fit for a princess."

"Yes," Jean said dryly. "But she didn't really consider herself a princess anymore."

"Well, let's see if we can find one that Stephanie would have picked," I suggested.

We walked together around the room until we came to a smoky purple one in the same design as Steve's and Greg's.

"How about this one?" I offered. "Her favorite color is purple. But it's not too purple."

Jean studied the box and was satisfied. "It does look more like what she'd pick. What do you think, George."

George nodded his approval.

Jean wanted the spray to be roses, red ones, to emulate a painting Stephanie had done in art class of a red rose on a background of black. I remembered how proud Steph had been when she brought it home from school.

"I made it for Mom," she said with a smile of satisfaction. "She likes roses."

I was glad the painting meant so much to Jean. It was made with a lot of love, and for the past twenty days Steph was that single rose in a background of darkness. Yes, the rose was an appropriate flower for Stephanie.

Jean didn't know what to do about a dress for Steph. She didn't think she wanted to bury her in the dress she had bought her for the kids' funeral although it was beautiful, of black silk with a sea gull soaring in a shadow of pale blue.

I remembered the dress Stephanie wore back to the hospital after her weekend home. It had a colorful floral pattern with a hood. Steph had bought it with her first paycheck from working at the police chief's office. It was her favorite. I told Jean it had to be among the things she took home from the hospital. Jean remembered seeing the dress and agreed to use it.

* * *

That evening we held a visitation at Mount Moriah. The casket was open. Steph's long blonde hair had been teased and brushed till it looked full. The hood of her dress was raised loosely around her head with the hair flowing out around its edges. A light touch of makeup had been applied, and her fingernails had been manicured.

She looked so beautiful and healthy now. The swelling was gone, and her color actually looked better. A violet pillow cradled her head. Harry T. Hound and the Unnamed Lamb were propped into the corners of the casket. It only seemed fitting that they go with her.

Stephanie took her place beside Steve the following afternoon, under the shade of a single billowy cloud that seemed to hang just above the graves. The burial was like a quiet sigh after all these weeks of turmoil. For the kids, the ordeal was finished. I said my last good-bye silently.

As the crowd faded away, George and I walked around the canopy to spend a moment with the other four. As requested, four little bouquets blew gently in the wind, like a parade of marching soldiers in perfect formation. Six carnations apiece in pink, yellow, orange and blue were the only markers on the unsodded graves. "We are marching to Zion," they seemed to be singing. "And Stephanie's going with us."

We walked away alone, up the hill to the funeral home. Halfway there I looked back at the billowy cloud. It had broken into four pieces and was drifting up to heaven. Had the kids come to watch their sister's passing? Or was it their guardian angels? Only God knew for sure.

We received a letter in the mail that day from a resort owner friend. She had been in the hospital for minor surgery the week Stephanie was admitted and visited with her twice while there. Though we didn't know her well, her letter reflected the sentiments of many.

Dear George and Joy,
There's not much left to say, is there? I'm sure you've heard over and over again how much better off she is now that she isn't suffering any more. That always seems to be the comforting thought people tell you at times like this. This loss, added to the others, just staggers the imagination, and if there are any right words to say I'm afraid I won't be the one to say them, as my mind is being kept busy just trying to absorb everything and find an answer to it all.

This chapter in your lives has been as dark as anyone could imagine. This is all behind you now, and I know nothing the future could hold will ever be as dark. I hope the remaining chapters are filled with love and laughter and that you'll be able to find the strength to pick up the pieces and go on.

I'm glad fate saw fit to bring us together, and all my thoughts in this letter I'd like shared with Jean, who has suffered as much, but I'm sorry, I don't know how to reach her.

I guess when we realize they are all together now, without worry or pain, it's easier to go on. So I wish I knew why I keep crying. I hope the enclosed poem doesn't upset you, but I had to put my feelings down. I'd love to see if I could get it published so there'd be something permanent for Stephanie. Despite the tragedy of the others, she suffered the most and the longest.

As ever,
Carol Farrand.

I pulled the spring green paper from the envelope, and unfolded it carefully, wondering what kind of a poem might do Stephanie's life justice. But as I read the words, I knew that Carol had caught the essence of our loss, and the tragedy of Stephanie's trials for all to see.

Stephanie

This should have been the beginning for her:
 Parties, proms, secret loves,
 Rap sessions with her friends.
 Instead her days were filled
With needles, and tubes, and hospital beds,
 and pain.

 And her secrets were shared
With a brown and white stuffed dog.

 And the doctors attended her,
 The nurses cared for her,
 Her family comforted her,
 And everyone prayed for her,
 But we couldn't cure her.

And the feeling that hurts the worst
 Is knowing Stephanie died
Before she had a chance to live.

Carol Farrand

Chapter 15

===========

New Hope

Saturday morning George and I packed a single suitcase and pointed the truck west. We needed time alone together, time to quit worrying about comforting others, time to heal before I went away. I dreaded having to check in at the hospital, scared to death I would never come home again, wherever home was to be.

As the miles separated us from the city, the confusion of the last few weeks began to wind down. On the seat between us was a brand new 35mm camera with an extra 200mm lens.

Many people had walked up and handed us money rather than giving to the memorial funds set up now in six lake area banks and two Kansas City ones. Don Turner oversaw the lake funds, and collaborated with an officer friend named Roy Miller, who was handling the Kansas City funds. The money would be used to help pay for the funerals and other expenses involved in the kids' deaths.

But this cash money was to be used for our expenses, people said, to help us in our transition back into life.

"Spend it on something foolish," one man said. "Go buy yourself something you've been wanting for a long time."

So that's just what we did. George had been wanting a camera that would take good wildlife shots for a long time. The new hobby would help to keep our minds occupied. Our days had been so empty lately.

Now we were heading out to the endless fertile fields of Western Kansas, where we hoped to get some great close-up shots of pheasant and mule deer. But more than that, we just needed to hide in the corn and wheat fields–to run away from our grief for a while.

George was good at that. All his life he'd tried to walk away from trouble and run away from hurt. To put distance between himself and his enemy. He couldn't run to the Ozarks this time. He had to run the other way. Western Kansas was the only other place he knew.

The deaths of the children made us realize how fragile and vulnerable the human body is. Now each day together was a victory against death, and each tomorrow, the start of another round. Neither of us knew when the fight would be over, or who would be the winner, but that word cancer droned in our heads and threatened to tip the scales in death's favor.

The ribbon of highway cut through fields of corn, wheat and milo, drawing us closer to the earth. The sunset that evening flashed pink across the clouded sky in a dazzling display of nature's grandeur. As my world darkened, the world in which God lived was radiant with light.

Not once in the seven-hour journey did a child pop up from the back seat with the words, "Dad, how many more miles?" or "I have to go to the bathroom." The ride seemed peaceful, yet eerie without it. It had been so long since George and I were truly alone.

The moon shone bright above us as we pulled into the drive of the Nipps' farmstead just outside of St. Francis. We were welcomed by Ol' Dink, a mongrel cowdog that was already old a decade before.

George had come to hunt pheasants for fourteen years straight at the Nipps' farm. The hunters always stayed in the original homestead on the farm, an ancient two-story house that Hookey Nipps was raised in, but stood vacant since his parents passed away. He and Dee built a newer brick structure after they were married, and raised their only son there.

For fourteen years during the pheasant season, George had watched little Charlie grow up. He'd missed the last four years, for lack of money. Charlie was married now, and lived with his wife and two toddlers in a basement house on the farm. Dee insisted we stay in Charlie's old bedroom. Though I had never been here, she welcomed me warmly into her home.

We spent the next day bumping down the back roads in search of game. I lost myself in the moment, forgetting the past and the future completely, and pulling George with me into the tunnel of now where it seemed safe for a while.

We explored an abandoned homestead and caught a few glimpses of mule deer on film as they peered through the tall grass of the untended field and then bounded away. I turned just in time to catch a pheasant in flight, and the new camera stopped him in mid-air. A beautiful sharp clear print.

George took pictures of me sitting on the hood of the truck looking out over the fields, and others while I wasn't looking. Preserving these moments just in case they were our last. After dinner we strolled across the fields of corn stubble together.

Tomorrow we would return to the city, to hospitals and relatives, and grieving people. But tonight it was just me and my love, standing in a corn field without a care in the world. I wanted to stay here forever.

* * *

Tuesday morning I packed slowly, in no hurry to get to the hospital. George checked me in while they did blood and urine tests. I had always prided myself in being a model patient, but the memory of the tests Steph went through invaded my thoughts. For a moment I panicked.

"Calm down," the nurse said. "We're just taking a blood sample. It's very routine."

I knew that, but I was scared to death what they'd find in it.

George was scared too. I didn't really know which one of us had the worst of the deal—the one contemplating death, or the one contemplating life all alone buried in grief. I wouldn't have traded places with either of us.

Today was just a preliminary day to get ready for the surgery. I was given a room on the second floor. George helped me settle in and stayed with me the rest of the day.

Dr. Horseman came to my room that evening to tell us what he planned to do. He would cut a cone-shaped section out of the cervix, slice the specimen into ultra-thin sheets, and examine them under a microscope to determine if cancer cells were present. We would go from there. It sounded horrible to George, but anything medical sounds horrible to him.

A nurse came around at eight o'clock and shooed George out. He returned to Mom and Dad's apartment to sleep alone. I didn't sleep a wink thinking about what tomorrow would tell.

Wednesday morning George got to the hospital well before the surgery. Dr. Horseman came in to make sure we were doing okay, and then ordered the nurse to give me the first injection that would put me to sleep.

"This is it," my mind kept saying. "This is it."

The nurse raised the needle and tapped the side of the tube to release any air. The drug entered my hip with a pain I can describe only as if someone had grabbed my innards and was pulling them out through that tiny hole. I tightened every muscle and shuttered out of control.

"You've got to relax," the nurse insisted.

My thigh cramped and I started to scream. I'd never been so frightened. George held my hand and squeezed it tight until the cramp eased.

I looked to the window as a possible escape. "I can't even jump if I want to," I grumbled.

The window was blocked with decorative brick. Nothing larger than a cat could be tossed between the holes. Besides, a two-story fall wasn't enough to do any more than complicate my medical condition.

"Just relax," George said. "Everything's going to be fine."

I wished I could really believe it. The nurse left us alone once more. I lay in the stark white bed and breathed deeply to stay calm. George kept my hand in his and tried to focus his attention on the talk show on TV to put the present out of his mind.

The nurses came and put me on a gurney the way I'd seen them do with Stephanie so many times in Columbia. "This is it," my mind said again. We began the journey down the hall. George stayed beside me all the way, and kissed me quickly before we departed through the big double doors. For a moment he just stood there and stared after me, collecting his thoughts.

I have no idea how long the surgery lasted. I was still groggy when they wheeled me toward my room. A familiar hand slipped into mine. I looked up to see George smiling down at me. Dale walked beside him.

"Dale," I said. "Thanks for coming." It was all I could muster, I was still so drugged. I closed my eyes again as they wheeled me to the elevator, and down the hall.

God, I was glad Dale came to help George through the hours of waiting and not knowing. Dale always knew when George needed his friendship the most.

Dale and George were the only two people I knew who could ad-lib one-liners at will. George could start a joke and while everybody else was just keying in, Dale had already caught on and finished it for him. They had more fun that way.

It was weird, though. The morning after the kids were killed, Dale woke up with an urgency to come to the Ozarks. He knew that somehow we needed help, but had no idea why. He didn't go to work, but packed a suitcase and headed our way.

A few miles out of town, he heard about the kids on the radio. He turned around and went back home to await George's call. He knew we wouldn't be home and wouldn't know where to find us. But how did he know his best friend was in trouble?

Dale's five-year-old son, Little Dale, used to pick wildflowers with Tonya and bring them to me to decorate the dinner table. He and Tonya had plans to marry when they were older; they looked so cute together.

When Little Dale saw the news on television with Tonya's picture, he turned to his mother and said, "Mama, I lost my wife."

They had stopped in a field on the way to the funeral and let Little Dale pick a bouquet of wildflowers to give to Tonya. She had been buried with them, beside the rose and pack of chewing gum.

Dale stayed long enough to keep George company while the anesthetic wore off. Then he wished me well and scooted on home for supper. George watched me eat dinner, satisfied that my healthy appetite was a good sign. Pleading starvation, he left early and stopped for a bite to eat on the way home.

* * *

The following morning, Dr. Horseman strolled cheerfully into the room.

"Well, young lady," he said in a deep professional voice. "We did find cancer cells."

For a fleeting moment I panicked again. "This is it. Another nightmare." I wasn't going to be able to handle this.

"But it was so minute that when we cut out that little cone," the doctor held his fingers together to demonstrate, "it appears we got them all."

A thousand-pound weight was lifted from me. "Then I'm okay," I nodded.

"It looks like," the doctor confirmed. He pointed a finger at me. "But I want you to make sure you get a pap smear every six months for a while, just in case it wants to come back. And no more birth control pills! We'll discuss some other options after you've had time to heal."

George was grinning from ear to ear.

"One more thing," he said, turning to the door. "If you're planning on getting pregnant, don't for at least three months. Let's give that cervix plenty of time to heal."

"Yes, Sir!" I saluted.

He sauntered down the hall, humming some opera tune.

George gathered me in his arms and hugged me tight. Satan wasn't taking this one away from him yet! We wouldn't let him win this round.

"George, I want to have another baby," I cried. "I'm too young to go through life without children." Not until my reproductive organs had gone through the fire did I realize it.

"Oh, Punkin, so do I." George rejoiced.

Life suddenly looked brighter than it had in weeks. We had a future to look forward to. Maybe someday we'd be a family again. But our lives would never be as full as they once were. Too big of a chunk of it had been torn away, and could never be filled again.

* * *

I had to stay one more day to recover from the surgery. After George left I watched television to keep my mind occupied. But a sound coming from down the hall invaded my senses.

A faint cry. Then another. It was newborns! I turned the television off to hear more clearly. Yes, babies were crying in the hallway as they were being taken to their mothers to be fed. I was only a few doors down from the maternity ward!

I sat up in bed and strained to hear every shrill, dramatic, pathetic, hungry cry until the halls quieted at last. I imagined the newborns in their mothers' arms being fed.

I'd heard that one of the mothers had twins. I imagined her now trying to juggle two beautiful babies at once, and wished I could go and help her with one of them. I ached to experience the gentle touches, the eye contact that formed a special bond between mother and child, the wonderful smell of powder and milk.

But none of the babies here belonged to me. What was I doing here so close to the new mothers? I wasn't one of them. All my children were dead. I could never touch my babies again.

I pulled the family portrait from the bedside table to admire the beautiful faces of my children. I held the picture close against my cheek and spoke softly to it, needing to hold them so badly. Tears filled my eyes till I couldn't see anymore. They fell on the glass like rain.

My insides ached with emptiness, a pain worse than starvation because there was no way to satisfy it. My heart would never be as full as it once was, and I wasn't sure I could learn to live with the emptiness, it hurt so much.

How could a new baby fill the tremendous chasm left by the deaths of the others? It would be impossible. Ten babies couldn't begin to fill it.

I actually considered the idea of digging up the children and taking some body tissue from each one. I'd read in a magazine that scientists were studying the possibility of using body tissue to create an exact clone of that person. The kids would be just like they were before. They'd grow up all over again.

But then I thought of all the experiences we'd had together. What happened in their lives played a vital part in their developing characters. It would be impossible to duplicate their lives completely.

Besides, if they were cloned they'd all be "born" at the same time. It would be like having quintuplets, not the family we had before. Greg was so proud to be a big brother, and Stacy was just meant to be the baby of the family.

It could never be the same. It was all broken apart and nothing could be done to change it. It was all too ridiculous to even consider, but a grieving mother's heart will try anything to get her children back!

Why did this room have to be so quiet, I thought. I'd give anything to hear a familiar laugh. Just a chuckle. One more, "Hey, what's for dinner?" "Has anybody seen my baseball?" "Mommy, I need a drink."

"God, please bring them back," I cried. "I can't live with this emptiness."

A nurse walked by my door and heard me crying. She came in and sat beside me.

"Are you okay?" she asked.

"I don't know," I whimpered. "I miss my kids so bad."

She looked at the picture I held. "They're beautiful children," she said.

"They were the best," I sobbed. "But I'm never going to touch them again."

"You'll touch them again someday," she said. "The Bible promises that."

"But I need to touch them now," I whined. "How long do I have to wait? How can I be sure?"

"Well, the Bible says that Jesus is coming very soon, and when He does, you'll be with your precious children again."

"But when is He coming?" I asked.

"The Bible says only God knows the day. But we should be ready. The time is very near. All the signs point to it."

"Where does the Bible say this?" I cried. "I've been trying to find out, but I don't know where to look."

She took the Bible from the drawer and opened it to 1 Thessalonians 4. She placed it in my lap and pointed to verse 16.

"For the Lord himself shall descend from heaven with a shout, with the voice of the archangel, and with the trump of God: and the dead in Christ shall rise first. Then we which are alive and remain shall be caught up together with them in the clouds, to meet the Lord in the air; and so shall we ever be with the Lord. Wherefore comfort one another with these words."

I read through the verse a second time. Jesus was coming back to reunite us! I was going to see my children again amidst trumpets and angels! What a glorious sight that would be. What a reunion! My heart was filled with a hope I had never known before.

"You just keep looking in here," the nurse said. "And if you need somebody to talk to or have any questions, you just call on me. I'm a good listener and I've got a broad shoulder to cry on."

"Thank you," I said as she rose to leave.

I thumbed through the Bible the rest of the evening, searching for more verses in the New Testament that told of His coming. I found some fascinating verses on family life, standards of living, prophecies that Jesus fulfilled, and signs of Christ's return.

"This is a fantastic book," I thought. Why hadn't I read it like this before? I always thought I had to start at the beginning. It never occurred to me I could read passages in the middle.

I could not absorb it fast enough. I wanted God to be proud of me. I wanted to be ready when Jesus comes. My thirst for knowledge was unquenchable. I would seek, and I would find. I would make my kids proud.

* * *

I left the hospital the next day and returned to my parents' apartment. Mom and I spent our evenings looking through her photo albums and matching up the negatives to any that had the kids in them. She gave me all the originals and planned to get reprints as she could afford to for herself.

Most of the pictures weren't dated, so I set to the task myself. Some were obviously of birthdays and Christmases, and were easy to tell. For others I had to match houses with haircuts, seasonal clothing, and other details and try to generalize them with a month and a year.

Mom cried a lot as we went through them, but I didn't. I wanted to relish the moments depicted in these photos and memorize the children's faces for all time. I ran back and forth between the dining room and living room to share a special pose of Tonya with Pa or a happy time with George.

My greatest fear was that I would forget. God hadn't forgotten my children. I would not disappoint my children by allowing them to slip from my memory. My memories would have to carry me through all the years until Jesus came back. I looked with all my heart to that wonderful reunion day and prayed it would be very soon.

Chapter 16

Starting Over

As soon as I recovered from the surgery, George and I headed out to Western Kansas again and spent nearly a month with Dee and Hookey. Pheasant season had started and George was more than ready to hit the fields.

I stayed near the truck and took pictures as he hunted. His heavy boots crunched against the corn stubble as he zig-zagged through the rows. The first pheasant came out of some underbrush and sailed across the stubble. George aimed the shotgun and fired, sending the regal bird to the ground. I whooped in triumph.

George retrieved the rooster several yards away, picked it up by the head and swung it sharply to break its neck. Taking its life seemed to soothe the vengeance he held for Billy and this Ray we didn't know. He gave the bird an extra jerk as if to say, "I wish the neck I just broke had been theirs."

George bagged two more roosters that day, and I took plenty of pictures of him hunting and cleaning them. They made a great dinner.

But George did more than just hunt while we were there. Hookey and Charlie were busy building an access road between two fields to make it easier to get the machinery to the crops. George volunteered to drive the road grader, happy to be doing something constructive after so many weeks of idleness.

I sat behind him in the big cab, savoring the endless golden wheat fields and brilliant blue sky as we slowly traveled back and forth on the newly made trail. The big steel blade cut into the ground on either side of the bank to create drainage ditches to filter the irrigation water away.

I looked around the cab and figured out a way to get all five of the kids in with us. It would be tight, but we would all fit. I rode along contentedly, making up little comments or questions the kids would say if they were here, and watching for little things that might have caught their attention. A mouse scurried across our path. A big orange butterfly flitted past. What was that big red knob beside the seat for? How do you back this thing up? I was lost in my own little world, and all the kids were with me.

In the evenings Dee and I stacked photographs of the kids in order and put them into an album. Whenever I worked on the project I was happy because it kept me close to the kids.

I spent a lot of time sitting alone in a stubble field and gazing up at the sky, trying to catch a glimpse of heaven, or the children themselves. I'd pick out a big billowy cloud and imagine the kids lying on it, peering over the edge at me. I lost myself in fantasy. Reality still hurt too much to live it every moment. George said I looked like an alien out there, begging to leave this place and go home to my own planet. If a hand reached down to take me, he'd run out to meet it. He wanted to go, too.

* * *

When we returned to Kansas City, we were ready to start making plans for life again. With help from the police chief, George landed a security job for a construction company on strike. It was a good job to start with because it didn't require him to deal with customers or supervisors while he worked out his grief.

On December 1 we rented a house in Shawnee, a suburb of Kansas City, and retrieved our furniture from storage. I wanted to set up the extra room off the garage as a memorial to the kids. But friends and relatives didn't think it was a good idea. They said it was time to bury the past and get on with our lives. They couldn't know that it would never happen.

"We've got a little problem," the man at the kennel told us when we called long distance to make arrangements to retrieve the dogs. "A man came in last week to ask about the setter. His daughter's setter was hit by a car. I gave him the dog with the understanding that he'd have to give her back if you wanted her. He paid for her shots and everything."

"I don't care what he paid for," George told him. "I want my dog back."

"I'll give him a call right now," he promised. "But you know, it's been over two months now that we've kept these dogs. I didn't know if you were coming back for them or not. Call me back in an hour."

When we returned the call he was quite distraught. We were told a Mr. Frieze refused to return the dog. George demanded his phone number and called.

"Hey, look," Mr. Frieze pleaded. "The dog sleeps with my son."

"You look here," George said. "That dog is the only living thing I have left of my son. And I want the dog back."

They argued for an hour. George was determined to win. Finally Mr. Frieze agreed to a trade. If we brought him a replacement setter, a female of not more than one year of age, he'd give us back Robin. What a sweet guy!

My anger got the best of me. I started plotting ways to kidnap the dog. George got out the newspaper and found just what we were looking for, a female Irish setter six months old.

The next day we bought the dog, named Dublin, for fifty dollars and headed for Camdenton. We didn't tell her owners she was going to be used as ransom to get our own dog back. Dublin didn't ride well and got sick all over the back seat.

When we reached Camdenton, we stopped at the kennel to get Lucky and then called Mr. Frieze. He gave directions to his ranch and said his son would meet us at the gate. It sounded like a big place.

A young man of eighteen or so, with the physique of a football player, was leaning against a jeep when we got to the gate. I wondered if this was the son Robin slept with, the one who couldn't bear to give up a dog he'd known for seven days.

He escorted us down the long winding driveway to the manicured lawn of a beautiful bi-level home. I held Lucky back while George put a leash on Dublin and led her to the door. When we walked in, Robin was sitting at the top of the stairs.

"Come here, Robin," I coaxed her. "Come on, girl."

She hesitated a moment, then quietly picked her way down the stairs. I petted her lavishly and rubbed her curly floppy ears. She reached out her paw to shake. She looked so sad.

The boy unhooked Dublin's leash and patted her rump to make her go downstairs. No fanfare, hardly a word over the new dog. Dublin was met at the bottom of the steps by two more Irish setters! I shook my head in disgust. Mr. Frieze was giving us all this trouble about Robin, and he already owned two setters. We took Robin and left quickly.

Lucky acted like an idiot when we opened the car door to let Robin in. Robin perked up at the reunion and the ride home was cheerful. At least we had some part of the old family back.

Robin groped about the house as if she could smell death on the furniture. She searched under things seemingly looking for the kids. Happy-go-Lucky acted like he didn't know anything happened at all.

George didn't get off work until three in the morning. Most nights I waited up for him. We'd eat dinner at four and then crawl into bed around five to sleep away the day.

I occupied the lonely evening hours by going through boxes of the kids' things. Several times a night, I'd call George at work to tell him about something special I'd found. Phone calls were one of the freedoms we enjoyed most about George's job. It gave us a chance to keep in touch whenever the need arose.

Over the weeks I made dozens of little discoveries to reveal the way certain things were when the children fell. Because we still knew little of what actually happened, we used each new piece of evidence to try to re-enact what might have happened. There just weren't enough clues.

One night I called to tell him I'd found Stacy's blue punch balloon, popped and spattered with blood.

"Whose blood?" I wanted to know. "Where was the balloon when we left that night?" We couldn't remember.

Another night, I was going through a box of Stephanie's old school papers when I dropped a piece of paper between the cracks in the cushions. When I couldn't reach it with my hand, I dropped to my knees to look under the couch. Directly below the place I'd been sitting, I saw a mark where a bullet had ricocheted away. A bullet aimed at Steve. I felt paralyzed by the sight.

Close examination showed that our chest of drawers had tiny droplets of blood sprayed across the drawers and mirror. Tonya's, no doubt, though she died a full three feet from where it stood. It's hard to look at blood and know it belonged to your child. One part of you wants to reject it. Another part wants to cling to it as a tangible piece of someone you loved.

Once we had all the kids' things together in one room, Jean came over to go through them. She took the chess set Steve made in shop class, and Greg's entire Matchbox car collection. She already had some of Stephanie's dearest possessions because she had taken them home from the hospital.

We borrowed a box of photos from Jean and had hundreds of reprints made showing the kids when they were younger. George and I worked together to label them and put them in an album. Our photographs were our most prized possessions.

Late one evening, I was thrilled to find two cassette tapes in a box I hadn't gone through before. The first one, Steve had taped at the family supper table, unbeknownst to the chattering brood. The other was taped by Stephanie during a family discussion on whether we could tighten our belts enough to afford a boat we were looking at. I called George at work.

"Oh George," I giggled. "It's so good to hear their voices again. You've got to hear these tapes."

We stayed up all night long to listen to them.

I never did get to set up my memorial room. By the time I got through all the boxes, I was feeling sick in the mornings. A visit to Dr. Horseman confirmed I was pregnant, and I hadn't waited three months.

On December 13, we learned through the newspapers that the juvenile court had waived jurisdiction over Billy Dyer. He would be tried as an adult, charged with four counts of capital murder. For this we felt victory. At least now justice had a chance.

* * *

The Christmas season came, and with it the quiet loneliness of a childless home. We decorated a tree as usual, but without tinsel, for there were no small hands to toss it in clumps about the room. I bought George a train set, just to have a toy under the tree.

On Christmas Day, George traded shifts with the day security man who still had young children at home. I spent the day at my parents' place, needing more than ever to be with family. All of the relatives smothered Jack III with presents, since he was the only grandson left on the Kirkham side.

George got off at seven and joined us for Christmas dinner. He was quiet throughout the meal, and only half-heartedly opened his presents from Mom and Dad. He just wasn't into the holiday spirit like he used to be. The relatives all thought he was handling his grief quite stoically. Though he talked about the kids freely, he rarely showed any strong emotions. None of us realized he was still in shock. George called me from work one night in January. His voice sounded funny, like he'd just come out of a fog.

"I was just sitting here," he said. "And I realized I just came out of shock! I have been in shock for four months and I didn't even know it till just now."

Being out of shock didn't make the grieving any easier for him. It opened up new emotions that were easier kept in check before. Sometimes the grief overwhelmed him now and he'd call me from work just to cry it out. Our ability to communicate was the one thing that kept us going.

As the months rolled by we learned to laugh again, to share happy memories, and to work out our guilt for failures to each other and the kids. We'd grown used to living with aching hearts, and the ache seemed almost normal now. But there were still so many questions, and without answers we could never fully heal.

Chapter 17

Preliminary Hearing

W hen a crime is committed, and the criminals are caught, we innocent victims foolishly believe the police are on our side and will provide us with all the facts they discover pertaining to our case. This just goes to show how foolish and innocent we are.

The authorities never really told us anything about our case. And as much as we disliked the ambulance-chasing, sensationalizing media, we discovered the media would provide us with the only real answers we would ever get.

We learned after the fact, via three different newspapers, that on January 23, 1978, a preliminary hearing was held for Billy Dyer and Ray Richardson, Jr. to determine whether there was sufficient evidence to hold them pending a trial.

Those three newspapers, the *Kansas City Star*, the *Springfield News-Leader*, and the *Camdenton Reveille*, provided us with the only information we received of the hearing and gave us the first clues about what really happened the night the kids were killed.

Billy and Ray were represented by two attorneys each. Ray's parents and grandparents pooled enough money to afford a couple of high-powered attorneys from out of state. Billy's were appointed by the court.

I'm sure there are some very fine defense attorneys in this country, men and women with conscience and diplomacy. But anybody who would try to get a killer off, knowing he is guilty, definitely has a problem with priorities.

None of the defense attorneys would go so far as to insist their clients were innocent. Their only line of defense was to discredit any witnesses, evidence or collection and analysis of such that was presented by the prosecution.

Among those who testified at the hearing were Robbie and Dan, the two eighth-grade boys who heard Billy brag about his plans to kill our family. Ray's attorney asked the boys if they ever heard Ray talk about plans to commit the crime. Since neither of the boys even knew Ray, they had never heard him talk about anything. The defense insisted this was clear evidence that Ray wasn't involved in the crime.

Yet when the prosecution asked the boys whether Billy Dyer said anything about his plan to commit murder, or whether he mentioned Ray in his plan, the defense objected that the boys' statements were merely hearsay and could not be used as evidence. In other words, no evidence was proof of innocence, and real evidence was hearsay.

The prosecutor presented a stack of photographs taken of the children as they were found after the killings and asked that they be entered as evidence. Ray's attorney wouldn't hear of it. He leaped from his chair.

"Your Honor, we must object to these photographs! Their only purpose is to show that the children are dead. We believe that an autopsy will prove that better. The pictures will only prove to be inflammatory against the defendants."

Darned right! Seeing an infant lying in a pool of blood with two shots through her head could be very inflammatory. But that's exactly what they did to my baby girl.

The prosecution argued its own case. "Your Honor, we believe the pictures accurately show the victims of the crime."

They argued back and forth until the judge demanded order. "I cannot make a decision until I see them," he said. After examining them carefully, he allowed them to be entered as evidence.

More evidence was entered and more objections made. But by far the biggest stink was raised over the reading of Ray Richardson's own typed statement of what happened that night. The defense didn't want it read at all and tried to discredit it by grilling the sheriff about how the statement was obtained.

Was Ray made to stand during questioning, or did he sit? What time of day was it? How long did it take? Was he given a break? Was he hungry or thirsty? Was he threatened with harm or promised special treatment if he told? Did the sheriffs wear guns during the questioning? Were Ray's Miranda rights read to him and did he fully understand them?

The sheriffs who questioned him had been extremely careful, and the judge could find no reason not to allow the reading. It was through this reading that the newspapers were able to give us the basic details of what actually happened.

Following is Ray's statement word for word as Sheriff Whitten read it at the hearing:

"About a week ago, Billy Dyer talked about some guns he wanted to pick up, take, at Swift's house. I thought he was joking at the time. He said that if he had to kill them to get the guns, he would, but he would do it when the parents wern't (sic) home.

"On Tuesday, September 13, 1977, Billy mentioned he wanted to look for his dog Daisy. We went down by the Lindsey Estates on State Road 'EE'. We stopped at a copple (sic) of trailers. He then asked me to drive up by the Swift's (sic) house. He knocked at their door and went inside.

"He told me that if they wern't (sic) at home, meaning the parents, he was going to steal the guns. He came back out a few minutes later and told me that the parents were at home, and that he couldn't get the guns.

"On Wednesday, Billy came over to my parents house and wanted me to drive him to the Swift's (sic) house and I told him no, I was going to stay home.

"About 6:00 PM, Thursday, September 15, 1977, Billy came over after I pulled up to my home. I invited him in for supper and he came in. I was fixing chow mein for supper. I knew he liked it since he had eaten it once before with me. It took me about 20 minutes to cook and serve supper.

"At 6:30 PM, Hogan's Hero's (sic) came on TV and we watched that. At 7:00 PM after Hogan's Hero's, (sic) Billy took a dish over to his mother of the chow mein. He told her we were going down to my trailer to play with my dog 'Scotty'.

"Billy came right back and had me drive him up to the junction, Sportsman Resort road, the road to Kon-Tiki, and the road to Point

View. I dropped him off there. I went down the road by Kon-Tiki and that circles back on 'EE' and I sat there at the junction for about five or ten minutes.

"I got curious and drove up past the Swift's house, towards Point View Resort. I circled back on an old dirt road behind the Swift's residence and I stopped on the road at 'EE'. Billy came across the clearing from the Swift's house with a pistol in his hand. He said he needed help.

"I moved the car back on 'EE' and Billy was running back towards the house. I went around past the house and pulled behind the Larson trailer. I got out of the car, and met Billy behind the church, he was coming towards me from the Swift's house. He still had the pistol.

"We walked towards the right side of the Swift's house. Billy said, pointing towards a boy laying on the ground close to the house, and said something to the effect that he had to shoot him, or kill him, or something like that.

"We walked towards the front of the house. The little girl was running around out there screaming. Billy said he hit her over the head with the gun and told me the gun wasn't firing right. Billy asked the girl to get back in the house.

"She was yelling something to the effect, don't shoot anymore, don't shoot in the house. Billy told her to shut up. She kept saying don't shoot.

"Billy had gotten her in the house by now, and I was in there too. Billy picked up a knife somewhere, I'm not sure where the knife came from. Billy stabbed her, while she was pretty close from the front door, in the living room. He stabbed her in the chest. She fell to the floor, she either pulled out the knife or it fell out.

"I was standing in front of the kitchen table, close to the utility closet. She got up from the floor and ran past me. I noticed that the knife was not in her. Billy ran up and fired a couple of shots at her. She stumbled into the bedroom. I did not see her after she stumbled into the bedroom.

"Billy turned off the TV, he said something to the effect it was bothering him. Billy noticed that the boy on the floor by the couch moved, and he fired three or four shots into him.

"I saw the little child girl walking around in the living room and she was headed towards the bedroom. She was sucking on a little 'ducky' bottle, baby bottle. Billy reloaded the gun and he asked me to pick up the empty shells that had already been fired. I picked them up and put them in my shirt pocket.

"He handed me the .22 pistol. I was looking the pistol over. I pulled back the hammer and it hit the firing pin, causing it to go off. The bullet hit over by the bunk beds in the corner of the living room.

"Billy took back the gun, but before he took it back, he told me he had to make it look like a robbery. He started knocking things over in the living room and the bedroom on the left, as you walk in the house.

"Billy had the gun now. He shot a couple of times at the youngest one, and the baby fell to the floor. One of us noticed a car pull in the Swift's driveway. I ran to the bedroom on the right. I opened the window and Billy and I jumped out the window. Billy yelled something at me, I couldn't understand what he said.

"Billy and I ran over the bank and back to the car. We left and drove straight to my parents house. We pulled underneath the sun deck, on the water front side. Billy then shoved a bigger pistol towards me and he picked up the .22 pistol. Billy, when he shoved a bigger pistol to me said, 'this is for your help.'

"I left the pistol on the front seat of the car when I went inside the house, and Billy was walking towards the lake. I'm not sure he threw the pistol in the lake or dropped it in the Honeysuckle bushes on the bank of the lake.

"Billy came inside the house, upstairs to the kitchen. I had already turned on the TV. Billy stayed at my parents house until about 8:15 PM or 8:30 PM. Billy went over to his house then and came back about 9:15 PM or 9:30 PM.

"While he was over at his house, I washed my jeans. When he came back, he wanted me to come over to his house. His parents were gone to pick up Ron's mother. While me and Billy were over at Billy's house, Tiger closed up the lounge, about 10:15 PM. Jim Masso came over to Billy's house, gave Billy the keys to the lounge.

"After Jim left, I went and got the pistol that Billy had given me earlier, off the front seat of my car and threw it in the lake about 20 to 25 feet of water, a little bit left of a dead tree that was laying in the water.

"About 11:00 PM Billy's parents came back. I left then and went home. I went back over to Billy's about 15 minutes later, told his parents I was going to pick up my dog that was down by the trailer. I got the dog, came back to my parents and spent the night.

"While Billy and I were upstairs in the kitchen of my parents house, after we had come back from the shooting, I took the empty shells out of my shirt pocket and threw them in the trash can, the one we burn trash in.

"On Friday morning, September 16, 1977, at about 10:00 AM Billy rang the doorbell down by the lake front. I went down and answered the door and Billy wanted to know if I wanted donuts at his house. I went over to his house with him.

"While we were at his house, I mentioned I was going into Camdenton. Me and Billy left for Camdenton about 11:00 AM. We went to the Post Office, where I sent my electric bill in, then to WalMart, then to Camdenton Library. Billy got himself a library card. We came on back to Thriftway, picked up some groceries, and we got back to my parents house about 12:15 PM.

"Billy mentioned at this time he had accidently (sic) shot off his finger tip last night. He showed me the finger, I believe it was the middle finger on his right hand. It was black, about where the nail is, on the side of the finger.

"I fixed lunch, tuna fish, and Billy did not like tuna, so I ate. Billy stayed at my parents until about 1:30 PM. He then wanted me to come to his house and we went over there. His parents were home at this time. We stayed there until the police came."

As soon as the sheriff was finished reading the statement, Billy's attorney was on his feet to object. The judge overruled.

According to the pathologist, Tonya was found with what appeared to be a one-and-a-half-inch long, half-inch deep laceration on the left side of her chest. The prosecutor entered into evidence a steak knife found on the floor of the living room after the killings. Tests showed Billy's left thumb print on the blade of the bloody knife.

Though Ray Richardson's statement indicated exactly when and where Billy had stabbed her, the defense wanted to argue that there was no proof this particular bloody steak knife was the implement used to stab Tonya. Billy had been in our house many times before and could have left that thumb print anytime.

At the end of the hearing, Ray's attorney moved for dismissal because there was no physical evidence "to link Ray to the actual killings." The prosecution argued Ray lent assistance to Billy in the killings and was therefore guilty of the crime. Billy's attorneys also moved for discharge because the only physical evidence, the bloody knife, could not be positively identified as the one used to stab Tonya. Furthermore, Ray's statement was all hearsay, and reading it was a violation of Billy's right to confront a witness, they said. Without those two pieces of evidence, the state could not prove that Dyer was involved in this felony.

The judge weighed the arguments and decided in favor of the prosecution. He ordered both defendants bound over for trial, charged with four counts of capital murder.

* * *

There were several things about Ray's statement that bothered me. For one thing, Billy had come looking for his dog on Wednesday, not Tuesday. And while the pretext was to look for a lost dog, Ray knew Billy's real purpose was to commit robbery and murder. They had discussed it repeatedly.

Ray also went into detail about how he avoided parking near our home and took the time to hide the car behind the Larson trailer before coming to assist Billy, who was waving a gun when he asked for help. Ray knew it was no social call he was walking into.

In his statement, Ray concentrates on what Billy was doing, not on what he was doing. While it is not clear in the written statement, it came out in the sheriff's testimony that Ray admitted to checking the gun over when Billy said it wasn't working right.

According to police, seventeen shots were accounted for, twelve of which went into the kids. Ray admitted to firing at the bunk beds, and there was a hole in the wooden frame to prove it. One shot went into an inner wall, evidently aimed at Tonya as she stumbled toward the bedroom. One ricocheted off the couch. Two holes were in the front door, shot from the inside. Who fired the shots at the front door, and when?

Ray also mentions seeing Billy reload once, right before killing the baby. Yet, at least seven shots, and more likely eleven, were fired in his presence before then. The gun had to be reloaded between the shootings of Tonya and Steve. And no matter how many different ways I tried, at no time could I see Billy firing six shots in a row.

Billy came looking for Ray's help because the gun wasn't working. If it had been, Billy would have fired more shots than the two used to kill Greg and bring down Steve. Only two shots had been fired when Ray entered the scene. It stands to reason that Tonya was hit over the head and stabbed only because the gun wasn't firing. Ray looked at it. Did he unjam it, or reload it? In his statement, he doesn't say.

But after that, the shooting started again. Tonya took four. The wall got one. Ray said Billy then started firing at Steve. He would have had to reload. Three more went into Steve, one hit the couch.

Ray said Billy then reloaded and handed it to him. Ray fired a shot at the wall. Billy then took the gun and killed the baby.

Because the police were never allowed to question Billy, there was speculation about how Billy got the .22 in the first place. One guess was that he managed to con Greg into taking it out for target practice and, once outside, turned the gun against his friend.

I hated this idea. Would Greg have disobeyed everything he was taught and taken his father's gun out? And if the gun was in the freezer, how would they have gotten it past Steve without him seeing it? Steve would never have let them take it out.

Did Greg die feeling a last moment of guilt for betraying the family trust? If so, I wanted to somehow let him know I had forgiven him for his mistake. If only he could have come to me when Billy was trying to con him.

If Greg wasn't guilty, how could I clear his name? In spite of all that we knew, there were still so many questions left unanswered. The clues just didn't paint a full picture, and I desperately needed to know the whole story to satisfy my heart.

* * *

On February 10, a formal arraignment was held for Billy Dyer. He pled, "Not guilty by reason of mental defect excluding responsibility for his conduct." His attorney requested psychiatric examination. The judge granted his request and demanded he remain in custody without bond.

Through the psychiatric testing, he was found sane and competent to stand trial, charged with four counts of capital murder. In 1978, capital murder carried a penalty of life imprisonment without parole for fifty years or the death penalty.

As much as I wanted justice, I really didn't want either of them to get the death penalty. My reasoning behind this confused even me, since at the police station I would have gladly killed them, given a chance. Now I wasn't so sure.

According to Pastor Turner, if Billy and Ray were truly sorry for what they did, God would forgive them and allow them into Heaven. I didn't know that much about God to know how long He required them to be sorry, and since my kids had just gotten there, I wasn't ready for their murderers to make it to the Kingdom so soon. No, I wanted them properly punished for what they did.

Others told me the dead were asleep in the grave until Jesus comes. If that were true, then death would be too easy for them. Someday they would stand before God, but for now I wanted them to suffer and feel pain. I wanted them to experience a living hell on earth. I wanted them to know fear in prison, fear without escape, like my kids had felt. I wanted no mercy, for they had shown none.

I lay in bed at night wondering what they were doing in their jail cells. I was told the sheriff often went in and played checkers with Ray to keep him company. The very act seemed like a conflict of loyalties to me.

I dreamed up ways to get in to see them. "Give me five minutes alone," I would say. "I just want to talk to them."

When the guard was out of sight I'd pull a long heavy chain out from under my shirt. I'd whip them mercilessly as they cowered against the bunks. I'd make them beg the way Tonya begged, but I wouldn't stop.

I envisioned gangs of prisoners surrounding them and no one hearing their cries. I wanted them thrown into a dark, windowless cell. I never wanted them to see the sun shine again.

But I didn't want them dead. Not yet.

Chapter 18

Guilty

The strike at Tobin eventually ended, which would have left George unemployed. Instead he was hired on as a welder for the company at a much better hourly wage than the security position. I was thrilled with the change. I didn't want him working nights after the baby came. So far, the pregnancy had been uneventful, and we were both preparing for the new arrival with great anticipation. In my fifth month I began to hemorrhage. Not heavily at first, but by the third day the bleeding increased. George took the day off to take me to the doctor. Dr. Horseman examined me with great concern.

"If we don't take steps to prevent it, we may lose this baby," he said.

The news struck me hard. "Dr. Horseman, please, I can't lose number six. I won't bury another one."

"I'm going to give you a shot that will help prevent a miscarriage," the doctor said. "If there's something wrong with the baby it should have miscarried in the first trimester. I suspect it's that cervix. It may not have fully healed before you put the pressure of pregnancy on it."

I rolled over and took the shot in the hip.

"There now," he said. "I want you to go home and go straight to bed. Don't you get up any more than is absolutely necessary. And you call me if the bleeding gets worse."

George took me home and tucked me into bed. He carried the television into the bedroom, fixed dinner and came in to eat it with me. He was quiet throughout the evening. I had no idea of the turmoil he was keeping inside.

The next morning George stopped by Dr. Horseman's office on his way to work. He was so afraid I'd lose the baby. But he was even more afraid there might be something wrong with it, a handicap he couldn't deal with. If that were the case, he would prefer to lose the baby and try again. He didn't want any unnatural heroics to save a malformed child that nature would have rejected. And more than anything, he didn't want to have to make decisions like that.

Dr. Horseman assured him if the baby was deformed or severely handicapped, it would abort no matter what he did. He was sure the cervix was the culprit, and not the fetus. George left the office fairly relieved.

For six weeks George came home from work, fixed dinner, and sat in bed with me to watch TV. I kept busy with needlepoint kits and crossword puzzles. The house went to the dogs. Mom and Dad came over on weekends to help clean up and help me write out thank-you cards. We received over a hundred and fifty sympathy cards and letters, and I wanted to respond to all of them personally.

Don Turner sent us an account of how the memorial funds were distributed, along with a list of every donor–three typewritten double-columned pages of them. Over eight thousand dollars were collected in all. One thousand went to settle Stephanie's hospital bill, originally in the neighborhood of thirteen thousand dollars.

Mount Moriah gave us tremendous discounts on the funerals. They charged us the price of one casket for all four in the first funeral. The concrete vaults were also one for four. Everything but the hole itself was tremendously discounted, only because the backhoe work was done by a private contractor. Stephanie's funeral was also discounted, but not nearly to the extent of the other.

There were ambulance fees to transport the bodies and to take Stephanie to Jean's, the motel bill and long-distance phone calls made to relatives while there, and my doctor bill for the tranquilizer. Everything had been taken care of.

Looking down the list, I saw that nearly everyone who submitted bills offered discounts and several even put part of what they collected back into the fund. After everything was paid, only twenty-five dollars remained, which was credited to the Mount Moriah florist shop to buy flowers for the kids.

It didn't seem fair that the community had to pay for Ray and Billy's crime. But without their help George and I might never have recovered financially. If everyone had submitted honest bills without discounts, the total would have easily exceeded thirty thousand dollars instead of only eight.

A month and a half after the bleeding started, Dr. Horseman cautiously let me out of bed. But I had to take it easy and not strain myself. The hot summer days were miserable with only a box fan. Every evening George stopped at the quick shop and brought me home a strawberry milk shake. I was growing as round as a marble.

My due date was August 1, but when the baby didn't come, I became a walking bundle of misery. I lay at George's feet in the evenings and bellowed my despair. George patted my belly and assured me the baby would come when it was good and ready.

Four days later, Sandy Dey Swift pushed her way into the world. George beamed with fatherly pride as he unwrapped the pink flannel blanket to study this beautiful creature we'd made.

Her skin was so delicately rosy, with the perfect puckered mouth of a China doll. Fine peach fuzz blonde hair, and those distinctive Swift brown eyes. Her tiny curling toes and little clenched fists were perfect in every detail. George went home a very happy man.

A nurse checked my vital signs into the evening to make sure everything returned to normal after delivery. I was absolutely exhausted, though the labor and delivery had been a breeze. I kept falling asleep in little spurts. In the wee hours of the morning, Dr. Horseman was called back to the hospital. I was losing too much blood. George was also called back. I was so delirious I didn't even know he was there.

A nurse brought in a pint of blood and quickly piggybacked it into the I.V. of normal saline. I felt the cold blood enter my hand and turn my veins cold with it. I drifted off to sleep.

The next morning I felt great. George arrived carrying three pink roses in a slender white vase. On the card he'd written, "Three girls? I Love You. George."

The pediatrician came in later to report that Sandy had jaundice. I wasn't overly concerned. Tonya and Stacy both had jaundice at birth. But theirs was at level two. Sandy was at level six. He wanted to put her under a special light.

The next day Mom and Dad came to visit. Mom went down to the nursery to see Sandy through the window.

She returned quite tickled saying, "Oh, Joy, you've got to come see her. They've got her under the light. She's got a little mask on, and she's kicking her tiny feet. She looks so cute!"

I pulled on my robe and hurried down the hall. I was appalled by what I saw. My tiny precious daughter lay naked and crying in the bassinet, her little heels rubbed raw from kicking so hard under the intense light. The mask covering her eyes looked to me like it was attached with tape. It horrified me to think they'd rip that tape off of her head.

I pounded on the glass and motioned for the nurse to come.

"I demand to know what are you doing to my daughter!" I seethed. "Look at her. She's in a torture chamber!"

"No, she's not," the nurse comforted. She pulled an identical mask from her smock. "Look, it's made out of Velcro. It doesn't hurt her. It just protects her eyes."

"Why is she kicking so hard?" I asked.

"Because newborns are used to being confined in a small space. They don't like to be naked. That's why, when a newborn gets fussy, we wrap them up tight in a blanket. Sandy doesn't feel secure right now because she has too much space to move around. But she's fine, really."

"Okay," I said. "But, please, when she's finished under the light bring her to me so I can comfort her." I didn't ever want this child to know the pain the others went through.

From the very start George was determined he and Sandy were going to be best buddies. He perched her on his chest in the evenings and cuddled her against his beard. On Sunday mornings, to let me sleep in, he'd get Sandy out of her crib and together they'd watch old Gene Autry westerns and reruns of Abbott and Costello.

Sandy loved it. She soaked up attention like a sponge and smiled at every camera pointed her way. We told her stories about her brothers and sisters, and somehow kept the kids close to us even though they were gone. It wasn't fair that Sandy would never know her siblings, or that they would never know her.

* * *

Billy Dyer sat in his jail cell alone and annoyed with the police. He wanted to talk to the media, to proclaim to the world what he had done. But his attorneys and his mother refused to let reporters near him.

Billy paced the length of the cell, trying to come up with a way, any way, to tell his story. He requested a cassette tape recorder, and when the guard was away, he asked an inmate in the adjoining cell to play the part of the reporter and interview him.

In great detail, he told of the killings, how the children fell one by one. The blood and the gore, their faces when they were dying. He laughed as if possessed.

Sheriff Larry Whitten was just entering the cell area when he overheard Billy taping his mock interview. His voice seemed charged by some unnatural force. The sheriff paused to listen.

"They deserved everything they got," Billy cackled, "I'd do it again in a minute."

He went on to describe his original plan, which was to stay and wait in ambush for George and me to come home, so he could kill us, too. If he'd succeeded, he was going to go on a rampage and "kill a whole bunch of people" until he got caught.

As soon as he was finished taping, Sheriff Whitten hurried to confiscate the tape for evidence. Billy grew angry that he would take it so forcefully. From there on out, Billy refused to talk to "Old Sideburns." He would never make eye contact with the sheriff again.

The police knew Billy had a juvenile record in both Connecticut and New Jersey, which was why they were being so careful with him. But because he was under age, they could not gain access to those records to find out what he'd done. But Billy wasn't finished with his jail cell boasting. Whether he was telling an inmate or bragging to the guards, the sheriff got wind of just what kind of a boy he held in his jail.

Billy professed that he tried to kill two thirteen-year-old boys in New Jersey using a poison blow gun. He missed one boy by an inch, he claimed. The deadly dart was caught in a screen door as the boy narrowly escaped. Sheriff Whitten used this new information to justify trying Billy as an adult. Until this young man was locked up, he would continue to be a threat to society.

There were rumors that police found a copy of Helter Skelter in Billy's room after his arrest. I wondered if it was Charles Manson's senseless killing sprees that sparked Billy's desire to kill. Or did they only fuel a flame that had already been started?

Billy must have found jail life quite boring, but over the months he found new ways to amuse himself. According to witnesses, he wired his television to the cell bars, hoping to electrocute the guard. His plan failed. He soaked cigarette butts in a cup of water to extract the nicotine, and soaked a pencil in the poison. He then tried to stab a fellow inmate with the instrument and poison him to death. This plan also failed. Because he was already being charged as an adult for capital murder, the sheriff saw no sense in complicating the court proceedings. No charges were filed in these two attempts. But Billy's boyish pranks were always potentially fatal.

* *

In early September, we received a subpoena for Billy Dyer's trial set for the eighteenth of that month. The trial would be held in Warrensburg on a change of venue, at the request of Dyer's attorney, who felt the boy couldn't get a fair trial in Camdenton. He was probably right.

On September 8, one week shy of the first anniversary of the killings, Billy waived his right to a jury trial and went before the Johnson County Circuit Judge with his attorney. He pled guilty to two counts of first-degree murder in the deaths of Steve and Greg. The judge accepted his plea and the charges against him in Tonya's and Stacy's deaths were dismissed. The judge handed down the toughest sentence under the law for first-degree murder. Billy was sentenced to two life terms to be run consecutively and not concurrently.

When we got notice of the verdict, we called our attorney to ask him when Billy would be eligible for parole. For capital murder it was fifty years. What was it for first degree? He answered by letter.

"For a simple life sentence, there is no parole for ten years. In this case, a multiple sentence, it will take a considerable period of time before this defendant is eligible for parole."

I didn't quite know what that meant. But as far as I was concerned, he should have been charged on all four counts. If Tonya's and Stacy's deaths were erased from the record, then I wanted them back alive. How could they reduce the severity of the crime after it had already taken place?

I resented the plea bargaining, even if he did get the toughest sentence available. He didn't try to plea bargain with the kids that night.

How could the criminal insist on mercy after depriving his victims of just that? I just didn't understand the criminal justice system. I couldn't see where there was any justice in it at all.

When Sandy was six weeks old we were subpoenaed for Ray's trial, which was to begin on October 10, 1978. Dad was also subpoenaed because he identified the bodies. We planned to stay at the Warsaw cabin Mom and Dad had purchased that summer and commute the seventy miles to the courthouse.

None of us could afford to take a week off work, nor could we really afford the expenses involved in the trial. Mom wrote to the courthouse seeking financial help, but no assistance was available to us victims.

The cabin wasn't set up for cold weather use. Mom bought electric space heaters to take down with us. We packed plenty of blanket sleepers and comforters for Sandy and prayed for sunny skies.

Billy was transferred from the Missouri State Penitentiary in Jefferson City to the county jail as a possible witness. This caused a great stir for the media and community alike. So many people wanted to get their hands on him, particularly his neck. Both defendants were moved through a series of back corridors for their own protection. Interior windows were covered with brown paper to conceal their movements.

We met with the prosecuting attorney the morning before the trial. He called George into his office alone and shut the door. "I want you to be aware that I plan to enter photographs of the kids as evidence," he said. "The only way I can do that is to ask you to look at them and identify your children. I don't want you to go into shock on the stand, so I'd like for you to look at them now, get over the shock, and be ready for tomorrow."

He tossed the stack of photographs across the desk. On the top was a picture of Greg lying in the grass, his head covered with blood. It was the most merciful of them all. The others were far bloodier. George held back the tears as he sifted through the stack. His stomach retched at the sight.

"I'm sorry to do that to you, George," the prosecutor said. "But these pictures will show the jury just what was done to your children. A picture speaks louder than a thousand words. We've got to make them see past that innocent-looking kid in the suit tomorrow. Can you handle it?"

"Yeah," he squeaked, wiping his eyes with the back of his hand. "I can do it."

The prosecutor told Dad and me that we probably wouldn't have to testify, but he asked us not to attend the trial just in case we were needed. If we were present at any time, our testimony would be worthless. George would be the first witness called in the morning. Mom agreed to go with him and take notes in shorthand.

The sun was barely up when the alarm went off the next morning. Mom rushed to put coffee into a thermos for herself and George, being careful not to drain the pressure tank. The pipes had frozen during the night. George tried to get his curly hair to behave without a shower and pulled on his suit coat ready to go. I sat on the couch like a zombie, angry that Mom was going to the trial and I wasn't. It wasn't fair. I wanted to see the man who killed my kids, hear him tell me why he'd done it. But I was only a victim and had no rights.

An early winter chill nipped the air as they headed out the door. The gray overcast sky made the whole world look bleak. Dad took a bucket down to the lake and filled it with water to flush the toilet. This was going to be a real rip-snortin' day.

I moped around the cabin all day long. Dad knew I was near my breaking point and quietly kept his distance. The strain of the trial affected my milk flow, causing Sandy to become irritable. I gave her bottles of juice to compensate for the decrease of milk. I held her close, missing the other five so much my insides ached.

The courtroom was filled to capacity when George and Mom arrived, and the halls were congested with little groups arguing their opinions of the case. The judge entered the courtroom and the trial began.

Ray's attorney entered a plea of not guilty by reason of mental disease or defect. He announced he would seek acquittal for his client because ninety percent of the evidence in the case was collected with Ray's help.

The prosecutor announced he would seek life imprisonment without parole rather than the death penalty. After Billy was sentenced to life, he didn't think there was a chance in the world of getting the death penalty for his accomplice.

George was called to the stand. The prosecutor was kind with his questioning. George identified his .22 pistol and told the jury when and where it was purchased. He talked about what the family had for dinner that night, what time we left the house, and who was there when we left. Then the photographs came.

"Who is this child in the photo," the prosecutor asked about each one. "What is the child wearing? And is that what he was wearing when you left the house?"

George's voice cracked and quavered. It took all his strength to study the pictures hard enough to describe the clothes, there was so much blood. His eyes started to blink and twitch, a nervous habit he suffers from when he's very distraught or self-conscious. He shook his head to stop them, but they just kept twitching.

The pictures were passed to the jurors, several of whom found them too graphic to bear. That's exactly what the prosecutor wanted. Now the five women and seven men would look beyond the neatly dressed defendant to the horrible scene in our living room.

George studied the defendant only a few feet in front of him. This was the first time he had ever seen Ray Richardson beyond a newspaper picture of him at his arraignment. He was small for twenty-one. Skinny too. He had the face of a weasel, with eyes too small for his head. He slouched over the table and didn't seem to care what was going on.

George was surprised that the police didn't search him before the trial. He suddenly realized he could have carried a gun into the courtroom. It would have been easy to conceal a pistol under his suit coat.

"There I sat a few feet from my children's killer," he told me after the trial. "I could have raised the gun and shot him before anybody knew what happened. I could have done it!"

Ray was guilty, just as guilty as Billy, but we knew the jury would never be shown all the evidence to prove it. His attorneys were too slick for that.

Behind Ray, in the first pew, sat his parents and grandparents who, more than once, reached out to pat him or smile in encouragement. George said it made him sick.

George was questioned about other guns he owned: what makes and models? The defense tried to discredit him, make him look like some gung-ho survivalist.

Was it true he owned so many rounds of this ammunition and so many rounds of that? George answered honestly and calmly.

Ray's attorney had an inventory of every bullet in the house and was trying to persuade the jury that we owned enough ammunition to start a war–as if our owning guns was cause enough to expect our children to be killed.

I felt sorry for the guy, making a living defending the guilty and discrediting the innocent. What a horrible way to earn your bread and butter.

Debbie Ballentine testified later in the day, as did pathologists and other officials in the investigative field. The water patrol told how the guns were found in the cove in front of Ray's house. The defense argued that Ray's testimony led them to look for the guns in that cove, and were it not for Ray's help they would never have found the murder weapon.

Ray's cooperation was also credited for leading police to the spent shell casings in Ray's trash can and to an investigation into Billy's wounded finger tip in time to detect powder burns on it, which was at least circumstantial evidence that Billy fired a gun. The defense was actually trying to persuade the jury that Ray had done them a favor by being present at the killings, to provide police with the clues necessary to convict Billy.

The prosecution called all of its witnesses and entered all evidence on the first day. The next day was the defense's turn.

* * *

When George and Mom returned to the cabin that evening, I was still moping around. I shouldn't have been mad at Mom. She was able to give me details of the trial nobody else would. Still, most of the information I eventually received came from newspapers.

The next morning I made sure everyone else was as miserable as I was. I wanted to go to the trial, and I felt it was my right to do so. Mom agreed to watch the baby if George wanted to take me up there.

He didn't want to, but his life would have been pure misery if he didn't. After we got there, George refused to go into the courtroom with me. I met Debbie Ballentine in the hall.

"The place is packed," she said. "We'll be lucky to find a seat." We crammed into the second pew, right behind Ray's relatives.

Ray had taken the stand and testified on his own behalf that morning, though I arrived too late to hear him. It was the one thing I really needed to hear, and I resented that I missed it.

Debbie told me his attorneys had programmed him well. He played the part of a good little boy caught in a bad situation perfectly. When asked if he reloaded the gun, he declared, "No." When asked if he tried to stop the killings, he again said, "No."

"I was confused," he whined. "I didn't know what I was doing."

The jury may have bought it, but I knew better. Several vital points were missing from the trial: key points that might have swayed the jurors if only they had been told.

It really irked me that Ray's relatives were allowed to take the stand and testify as character witnesses after sitting through the whole trial, especially when my family was denied that same privilege.

The grandmother testified that Ray was a submissive boy, never assertive. He was always a follower, never a leader. Ray had learning and speech problems, and physical handicaps as a child. He was partially deaf in one ear.

The defense pounced on that one. Were the police aware of the hearing deficiency when they read Ray his Miranda rights? Were they certain he fully understood what was going on? Ray hunched over and smiled at his grandmother.

Ray's mother testified that her son really had no aspirations in life. He tried to join three branches of the armed services and was turned down. The main thing he enjoyed was going to a movie by himself or doing something alone. "He was always a cooperative and obedient young man. He always did as he was told."

I was outraged. Sure he did what he was told. He drove Billy up there. He unjammed the gun. He picked up the shell casings. "Let me tell them what terrific kids mine were," I thought. "Before her sweet quiet young loner helped kill them. My kids had aspirations in life! They would have been something!"

A psychiatrist for the defense took the stand, wearing a fine business suit and an air of professionalism. He testified that in his opinion, "Ray suffers from a schizoid personality disorder which indicates a person is withdrawn and has an active imagination and a tendency toward eccentricity."

The condition is not serious enough to make a person lose touch with reality, but he believed Ray suffered from a mental disease or defect sufficient to make him innocent under the law.

The psychiatrist for the prosecution was not so richly clad as his colleague. He seemed more easy going and a bit less professional. But I liked what he had to say.

He agreed with the schizoid personality disorder, but claimed it was merely a character trait or style of living, not a mental disease or defect.

On the third morning, the jury heard the final arguments. They were asked to consider each child's death separately, and were given several sentencing options for each one, from second-degree to capital murder. They went into deliberation at noon.

The jury returned at five o'clock with a verdict. They found Ray guilty on two counts of second-degree murder in the deaths of Tonya and Stacy, but not guilty in the deaths of Steve and Greg because both had been shot before Ray entered the scene. Never mind that Steve was still very much alive, or that Billy never would have committed the crime in the first place if he didn't have Ray's car to drive him there.

At the time, second-degree murder called for a minimum term of ten years and a maximum of life. The jury recommended the minimum sentence.

The judge sentenced Ray Richardson, Jr. to two ten-year terms to be run concurrently and not consecutively. His time served in the county jail awaiting trial, amounting to 416 days, was to be counted as part of the sentence. He would receive psychiatric counseling for his personality disorder while incarcerated.

I was not at all happy with the sentence. The two ten-year terms should at least have run consecutively. If they had sentenced Ray to twenty straight years without parole, I think justice would have pretty much been served. To me, the sentence was a victory for the defense.

Chapter 19

Outnumbered

Little Sandy Dey crawled across the soft emerald grass and stopped at Steve's grave to smell the pretty blue carnations. Her tiny pug nose wrinkled as she sniffed. She touched one of them lightly; she knew better than to pull on them.

On the move again, she plopped down on Greg's granite marker, its coolness relieving her diaper-padded bottom on such a warm day. She glanced behind her at the purple flowers, then leaned to sniff the vase of orange ones in front of her. She traveled on to the yellow ones, and ended with the pink ones at the other end. She sniffed them deeply and clapped her hands in delight, satisfied she hadn't missed a one.

There was no sadness in her innocent young eyes. She didn't know what lay under the soil beneath her or why the flowers were there. That knowledge would come in time, when she was old enough to understand.

Our visits to Mount Moriah had become a weekly event in her short life, and for now, she was content to just be here to enjoy the atmosphere of the place. We were determined she would know this place as intimately as we did, and tried to make it a positive experience for her.

But the strain of Ray's trial and the anguish I suffered over the lax sentences had taken their toll on me. Shortly after the trial, I was forced to quit breast feeding; my milk supply simply dried up. Sandy had a tough time adjusting to formula, and I resented Billy and Ray for taking yet another part of motherhood away from me.

My turmoil surfaced again a few months later. I started to hemorrhage again. Several visits to Dr. Horseman failed to stop the flow. We tried pills, shots, and even cauterization, but nothing seemed to work. Finally, the doctor asked me, "Have you tried going to church?"

The suggestion took me by surprise. I'd been studying the Bible on my own and with a lady who came to the house once a week. I was beginning to memorize the books of the Bible in order and had learned to use a concordance to find answers to specific questions.

My biggest concern was where the kids were, and when I would be with them again. I was also trying to find out more about God Himself. I really didn't know Him well enough to trust Him to my children's care, and I was depending on the kids to look after themselves.

I saw God more as the Wizard of Oz, breathing fire and smoke and demanding to be appeased and honored before He'd do anything for you. It didn't occur to me that even the real Wizard of Oz turned out to be quite sympathetic to human needs and more than willing to step in and solve them.

Whether I really believed at this point that God could heal me, I don't know. But after speaking to the priest of a nearby church and hearing the story in Matthew 9 about the woman who hemorrhaged for twelve years and was healed simply by touching the hem of Jesus' garment, I was convinced God could do the same for me if only I had faith.

We started attending Sunday services and soon after that, signed up for evening Bible classes together. We became members of the church and made plans to renew our wedding vows on our sixth anniversary.

Two vases, each holding carnations in pink, yellow, orange, blue and purple, decorated the alter in memory of the kids. Friends and relatives filled the pews. There was a reception afterwards with cake, champagne, and even gifts, all things we lacked for our first wedding. We even bought new wedding rings, simple gold bands, to represent the durability of our relationship. We had been tried in the fire and been found true.

God finally did perform a miracle for me. Nine months after the bleeding started, it simply stopped. Perhaps that's how long it took for me to truly appreciate God's ability to do anything and to have the faith to let Him.

The promise I had found in Mark 11 held true. "Have faith in God," verse 22 said. "Whoever says to this mountain, 'Be taken up and cast into the sea,' and does not doubt in his heart, but believes that what he says is going to happen, it shall be granted him."

With God's help I could accomplish anything, and when the hemorrhaging stopped, I knew I'd proven it. I memorized a special verse from a plaque I saw and recited it every time I needed a little extra courage to see me through.

"I shall live each day knowing that nothing could possibly happen to me today that God and I can't handle together." I believed it with all my heart and leaned on God for all my needs.

The evening classes brought me to a fuller understanding of God's true character. God was a father, in every sense of the word. Being a parent myself, it was a relationship I could understand.

I loved my children with all my heart and wanted only the best for them. I was no Santa Claus, though, and being older and wiser than my children, I knew peaches were healthier than candy.

I expected obedience from my children and disciplined them when they did wrong. But no matter what they did, I never stopped loving them, and always forgave them when they said they were sorry. As long as they learned from their mistakes, and tried hard not to commit them again, their characters grew and were sometimes better for the experience. Whether they were good or bad, my love for my children never wavered.

That was God. And I found that reasonable and fair. I was finally able to trust that God was capable of looking after my children in my absence. He knew how I felt about them because He felt the same way.

I had to come to grips with the fact that Billy and Ray were also God's children, and He loved them as much as He loved my children. They had done a horrible wrong against us, but if they were truly sorry and learned from their mistakes, God could and would forgive them. That was God. And it was reasonable and fair.

But when I read in the Bible that God expected me to love and forgive them too, I couldn't do it. Ironically, I found this information in the same place I found the faith to stop the hemorrhaging, in Mark 11.

"Therefore, I say to you, All things for which you pray and ask, believe that you have received them, and they shall be granted you.

"And whenever you stand praying, forgive, if you have anything against anyone, so that your Father also who is in heaven may forgive you your transgressions.

"But if you do not forgive, neither will your Father who is in heaven forgive your transgressions."

The very idea was sobering. I wasn't perfect. I had sinned. And I knew my Father in heaven would forgive me if only I asked. But I'd never committed anything as horrible as murder. Surely God didn't expect me to forgive that. That was a commandment they broke! Murder had to be the most horrible trespass of all.

God surely only meant the little trespasses, and I had no trouble with those. In fact, I could probably forgive those even easier after what I'd been through. I kept my cool when others grew impatient and mean. If a stranger bumped into me, or I had to wait in line at the check-out because the checker kept pushing the wrong buttons or a waitress messed up my order, I could smile and tell them it was okay. A minor inconvenience. I hope it's the worst thing that happens to me today. Nobody's perfect.

But when it came to forgiving Billy and Ray, I just couldn't accept that God would expect that much from me. Surely He didn't mean murderers. He couldn't possibly mean forgiveness for something of this magnitude. There had to be a limit to all this forgiveness.

I searched the Bible to prove my point. I couldn't find a single verse to back me up. Jesus forgave His own murderers after being tortured and mocked and left to die on a cross. My children had suffered a terrible, painful death. But no worse than His.

Peter asked Jesus how many times he had to forgive his brother for trespassing against him. "Seventy times seven," Jesus answered.

I read it; I knew God meant what He said. But I wasn't ready to accept it. I wanted to shove forgiveness under a rock and walk away. I still carried too much hurt and was still learning to get by without the kids on a day-to-day basis.

* * *

Just before Christmas of '79, George was laid off at Tobin with the rest of the crew. Most of the men went to pursue winter jobs in the West until Tobin started up again. But families weren't welcome on spot jobs, and George couldn't bring himself to leave me and the baby behind.

He helped Dale paint a house here and there, but there just wasn't enough work to support both families for the winter. Without a steady paycheck we couldn't afford the high cost of city living. I was pregnant again, and as much as I wanted to stay close to the graves, our dream had always been to raise our family in the Ozarks. For our own peace of mind, we needed a couple of hundred miles between us and Camdenton, where Billy's and Ray's families still lived. So we focused our attention farther south around Table Rock Lake and Roaring River State Park.

We moved into a log cabin a few hundred yards from the lake and spent our days hiking up on wooded Turkey Mountain or searching for Indian arrowheads on the fine sandy shore until I got too big to keep up. That summer was the hottest one on record in a hundred years, and the added insulation of the pregnancy made me miserable. I spent a great deal of time sitting in the lake to escape the heat and the sheer weight of the child.

Before the summer ended, I presented George with a big bouncing baby who didn't need a blue blanket to tell what he was. Matthew Thomas Swift had chubby clunky hands and an ornery look to his grin that said he was one-hundred percent boy. He came into the world looking like he was ready to take on the challenge. And there were those familiar brown eyes again.

At least now there was a son to carry on the family name. But I felt no glory in knowing that now my son, and not Jean's, would be given the firstborn rights of the family, the special heirlooms and mementos that belonged to George and his father before him. Those rights had belonged to Steve, and it was dreadfully wrong they were torn away from him.

August 21, 1982, blessed us with a third child, a boy we named Michael George who, from birth, carried the sensitivity of Steve in his rich blue eyes. Sandy celebrated her fourth birthday that month and Matthew claimed his second one. All three turned out to be August babies, though it was never planned that way.

Sandy and Matt were so excited when we brought Michael home. Daddy sat protectively on the couch while they took turns holding their new baby brother. I watched them silently, soaking up the moment, glowing with pride and satisfaction. What a joyous occasion, the birth of a brand new human being. My son. But past memories began to creep into our wonderful day.

Tears blurred my vision as I recalled Stacy's homecoming and how excited Steve, Greg, and Tonya had been that wonderful day.

How abruptly that happiness ended five years ago when they were killed. We never used the word "died" when we referred to them, because none of them had simply died on their own.

Left to themselves, they all would have lived. Outside forces killed them all. George and I hadn't trusted anyone but ourselves to care for the children ever since. Sheer survival demanded that we remain a close family, and we were.

I watched George with the kids, so tender, so fatherly, so patient. The tragedy, if anything, brought us closer, even though I couldn't imagine being able to love him more than I did. His eyes still sparkled in the same familiar way that always made my heart melt. But when I looked deep into those eyes, I saw the pain of a broken man.

On the outside he wore a smile, but that look deep in his eyes and the gray that had crept into his thick hair the last few years betrayed him. Nobody could see the deepest wounds except for me because I shared them with him. We had both learned to function in spite of the constant aching. We could smile and laugh and dream. But behind every smile was a tear. Behind every dream lay the despair of what could have been.

* * *

Our tenth wedding anniversary found us permanently camped on our own ten-acre parcel in the Ozarks. Home was a Coleman pop-up camper with a screened tent beside it to ward off mosquitos and flies at mealtime. The kids had celebrated their first, third, and fifth birthdays here in the camper, and their young bodies were tanned and healthy.

For our anniversary, I cooked fried chicken, potatoes, rolls, and corn on the cob over the camp fire and brought the feast down to the dock where George was working. The weekend regulars, mostly houseboat and cruiser owners, couldn't believe I really cooked it all on an open fire. We were kind of celebrities down there for daring to live in a canvas house with three small kids and no modern conveniences.

"You're that family living up there in the pop-up, aren't you?" a newcomer would ask upon overhearing a conversation.

They all passed our place on the way to the dock and couldn't help but see our camp. We kind of liked the notoriety and prided ourselves on escaping so many of life's trappings.

"My God!" one woman exclaimed. "I couldn't live without my curling iron!"

But I found the life gave me far more time to enjoy the kids and the outdoors. It doesn't take long to clean house when it's only three beds and a table. Rainy days did get monotonous at times, locked inside a canvas structure trying to keep three toddlers content and keep them from touching the sides!

George worked seven days a week for a pittance, but the kids and I were welcome to come down to the dock anytime we wanted. I took the kids to church every week without him, but he always asked me to say a prayer for him when we got there. Afterwards, we stayed for the potluck and then a group of us would go to the nursing home to sing. The elderly patients loved being with the kids.

The top students from each of the Christian schools in the Missouri district were invited to attend a week-long camp and tour the Missouri State Penitentiary where prison ministries were being conducted for the inmates. Two of my favorite girls won the honor in our tiny eleven-student church school.

Pastor Ron Atkinson and his wife were going to take the girls in their motorhome. They knew what happened to our family, and that Billy and Ray had been sent to the Missouri prison.

I asked the pastor to let me know what the prison was like. And if, by chance, he could find anything out about Billy and Ray, I'd sure like to know. I wondered if the prison ministries had touched them in any appreciable way and wondered if I really wanted it to.

During the tour, Mrs. Atkinson asked the guard if he knew anything about Billy Dyer.

"Billy Dyer is the youngest prisoner ever to arrive here at the penitentiary at the age of fifteen," he said. "He has been held in solitary confinement since he arrived. He eats alone, he is escorted alone to shower and to exercise. He is kept in confinement because the other prisoners would probably kill him if we put him in with the rest of the population. Even among criminals, the worst crime to commit is to kill a child, and Mr. Dyer killed four of them."

Mrs. Atkinson asked if he had an accomplice.

"Yes, he did," the guard answered. "Ray Richardson was kept in solitary the entire time he served here. He was a model prisoner and was paroled his first time up."

The news left me feeling betrayed. We never received any notice of Ray's parole hearing or of his release. As far as the criminal justice system was concerned, we, the victims, didn't count. It was the State versus Ray, and the State had decided he'd done his time.

Ray had destroyed the lives of four innocent children, yet he served less than seven years in prison for murder! I was still held in my own prison of grief, a grief that wasn't even close to scabbing over yet.

The issue of forgiveness came to the surface like a forgotten monster. Ray's release had kicked away the stone that had concealed it for so long. I'd managed to reach the point of feeling sorry for Billy and Ray because I knew the final judgment would fall on them, and they would face the destruction they deserved.

I didn't envy them. The death they had inflicted on my children was only temporary, and someday I would be reunited with my family again. But the death that would fall on Billy and Ray would be total permanent destruction.

I'd also reached a point where I could accept God forgiving them, if they were truly, heart-rendingly sorry for what they did. I trusted God to judge their hearts fairly, far more than I trusted the judicial system. But I had no idea where either one of them was on a spiritual level.

I knew I was supposed to love the sinner and hate the sin, and when I looked at God's whole big plan for humanity, I could. But when I looked at just me, and how my children suffered under their hands, my hate for them was intense. I didn't want Ray to be paroled so soon. I wanted him to be properly punished for his role in the crime, and I didn't feel he had been. He was free to marry, to raise a family, to be a grandpa some day, all things that my children would never do because of the crime committed under his hand.

Yes, I could accept his repentance and God's forgiveness. But I had a really rough time accepting that he could live a normal life after depriving my children of doing so. And so soon!

A few weeks later, the church showed a film about prison ministries for our Wednesday night Bible study. The film told about the Christian ministries being performed in prisons around the country, and the effects of Christ on the inmates there.

I thought of Billy and Ray throughout the film. Had they changed? Were they sorry for what they did or had prison life only made them worse? Did they have nightmares reliving the crime, or were they totally insensitive about what they'd done? Had they or would they find Christ? Did I really want them to?

An inmate was interviewed in the film. A young man, Tex Watson, one of Charles Manson's followers involved in the Sharon Tate killings. He admitted he was the one who killed Sharon Tate and the unborn child she carried. He said he was sorry for what he'd done. He hurt for the family of those he killed. If there was anything he could do to bring them back, he would, even if he himself had to die.

"But he couldn't!" my mind screamed. "There is nothing he can do, no matter how sorry he is, to bring back their lives! Nothing!"

I started hyperventilating from the rage inside. I couldn't unscramble the Christian feelings from my selfish human ones. Did Billy and Ray feel this way too? If so, how could I call myself a Christian and still hate them? Jesus didn't hate anybody.

But how could I love them after what they did? The blood of my children cried out to me. How was I supposed to feel?

"You must love your enemy. He is your brother," Jesus called to me. "You must love the sinner and hate the sin."

The words filled my brain and spread like a flood, drowning the hatred right out of me. I didn't want to hate Billy and Ray anymore. Yes, I hated the sin, with all my being I hated it. But I could no longer conjure up the hate for the sinners. God had taken it away.

* * *

We knew Ray would be on probation after his release, though we didn't know for how long. While on probation, he would have to stay in Missouri. I wondered how the Camdenton community would welcome him home if that's where he dared to go. Though I'd only seen him once in the courtroom, he seemed like the type that would run home to Mommy.

Not knowing him, I had no idea what six years of prison life had done to him, and I feared for our family's safety. The quiet grief I had learned to live with suddenly changed to inner turmoil. I didn't know what to do now that Ray was out. Suddenly two hundred miles wasn't far enough away to keep us safe.

George and I felt the need to run. The threat of being victims a second time was too strong for us to relax and just enjoy life. The murderers had taken more than the kids away, they had stolen our Ozark dream.

Where else could we go? Kansas always managed to offer George a job, but without hills and trees, it never felt right living there. We needed some place beautiful. Some place away. We searched the atlas for a new place to call home.

It was late October when the last of the furniture was sold. Dry crunchy leaves fell from the trees and blew into the back of the pick-up as we packed our camping gear and made beds for the trip. We'd bought a topper for the back and laid a piece of plywood across the rails to serve as a bed for all three kids. They were still small enough to fit the short way across. George and I would slide in underneath and sleep on the floor.

We stashed duffel bags in all four corners around the wheel wells, stuffed the kids into the truck, and headed west to the Rocky Mountains of Colorado. We were going on a fact-finding trip in search of a home.

Just outside of Colorado Springs, the foothills of the Rockies came into view. The rest of the trip was a feast for the eyes. The craggy red and gray mountains, splashed with the deep teal green of the pines, were absolutely breathtaking. We oohed and aahed for miles. The air was crisp and so thin we gasped after the slightest exertion. I'd never seen a bluer sky.

After three weeks in the pickup, we settled in a small town on the western slope of the Rockies, and George took a job at the parts counter of a car dealership. We told few people where we were and put the utilities in someone else's name to make it harder to find us. Being hard to find was growing more important to our mental well-being.

We liked the West and seemed to fit in with the lifestyle and the people, who were more concerned with the issues that were important to us: health, education and the environment. The people here tended to mind their own business, yet they were always available if you needed help.

Over time we felt like we belonged out West the way we used to feel about the Ozarks. But we never could seem to settle anywhere, somehow afraid to get too comfortable for fear someone would come and try to shatter our happiness. We found the West a vast frontier and kept moving from state to state.

A couple of times we got homesick and tried to come back to Missouri, but the murders had stolen the Ozarks away from us completely by now. Two hundred miles was no longer near enough to protect us. It now took at least a thousand. Instead of time helping us to get over our grief, it seemed it was only making it worse.

Chapter 20

But Has He Changed?

By September of 1987, we'd made our way north to Montana and had rented a house in a quiet mountain town between the Bitterroots and the Sapphires. We lived on First Street (the town didn't have a Second). Snow already covered the very peaks of the mountains and gave the valley a taste of winter to come. But it was still very much autumn on the valley floor.

The forest fires had raged out of control that summer and choked the atmosphere for every living thing. It was all the fire fighters could do to protect homes sitting close to the flames. The autumn rains brought welcome relief to the weary fire crews, and the valley seemed to sigh with gratitude.

We were teaching our kids at home now, not even willing to trust their care to the school system. The years had not eased our fears. On the contrary, time made us more wary of dangers. As often as we moved, home schooling was the most stable educational environment we could offer. The kids excelled in geography, having traveled through thirty-six states already.

It was our fourteenth wedding anniversary the day a young woman reporter from the *Springfield News-Leader* flew up from Missouri to interview us. The newspaper was planning a full spread of articles for the tenth anniversary of the killings.

I didn't mind sharing my anniversary with bad memories. Our wedding anniversary always carried mixed emotions of happiness and grief because four days later marked the anniversary of tragedy and the memory of roses left in the house after the kids were killed. The joy of receiving roses had died for me, and George had ceased giving them years before.

I fretted over what to wear for days. Nothing in the closet seemed appropriate.

"Throw on a pair of jeans and be yourself," George said. "You don't have to impress anybody. I like you just the way you are."

I picked out my best pair, threw on a colorful Western shirt, and waited for the reporter to arrive, still not sure I was dressed properly to meet her.

My anxiety melted away when Connie Farrow drove up in her rental car and stepped out wearing blue jeans and a sweatshirt. Her mid-length champagne blonde hair draped casually along her shoulders, and the ever-so-light touch of makeup put me at ease. I knew we'd get along fine.

Sandy was nine now, Matthew, seven, and Michael, five. Connie had never been exposed to home schoolers before. The kids proudly displayed their matchstick replica of Boonesboro Fort to the reporter and re-enacted the French and Indian War in the living room before her very eyes. Then we sent them to the backyard to play.

The interview felt more like a comfortable chat with an old friend, except this one took notes while we visited. After the interview, we all piled into our Ford Bronco and headed into town for lunch at the Coffee Cup Cafe.

Connie mentioned this was her first trip ever west of the Continental Divide. George didn't see why her visit had to be all work and felt it was our duty to show her the mountains. So after lunch we headed on up into the national forest to pan for gold in a sandy bend of the West Fork River.

The kids splashed happily about in the icy water, seemingly oblivious to the cold. But Connie noted that they never ventured out of our sight. Connie flew home the following morning with newfound friends and a plastic bag full of wet, sandy clothes.

The next Sunday edition of the *News-Leader* carried a full three pages about our story, consisting of four separate articles. We even outdid the Pope's visit to New Orleans! The first article was about us, what the past ten years had been like since the killings, and how we had changed—the fact that, in nine years, George and I had never left the children to go out (one of us always stayed with the kids, or we all went together); the need for so many miles to separate us from the tragedy; and our longing for a home.

The second one was based on interviews from people who lived in Camdenton and still could not forget the tragedy. It mentioned our house had burned to the ground a few years back, leaving only the front porch and foundation. Though there were rumors of arson, officials ruled the fire accidental.

I wasn't sad to hear the house was gone. I never could accept that someone was willing to live in it after what happened. To me, the house stood as a silent tomb in memory of the tragedy, and since the children who had brought life and joy to its walls were gone, it only seemed fitting that the house would die also. It was sort of a symbol of the last death, breaking our ties to the Ozarks forever.

A third article was a compilation of thoughts from a reporter assigned to cover the murders and Ray's trial. It offered a glimpse of the hardships and obstacles involved in covering the story. After reading it, I had new respect for reporters because through it all, they were the ones who ultimately gave us any information we ever received. His final statement about Ray's trial lingered in my mind for a long time.

"Down in a jail cell, Billy Dyer waited out of sight. But not all the time. A quick view of Dyer's unworldly, piercing eyes and a grin that still can't be described coming from behind bars is the one image that remains..."

The fourth article was the most interesting to me, for it gave me an idea of what the law enforcement officials thought of the case. The entire article was based on interviews with them.

From Sheriff Whitten: "At first we had people trying to get in jail to get to the suspects. In fact, we were asked, 'How could you bring them in alive?'" He said Billy Dyer killed the kids because he "thoroughly enjoyed doing what he did."

He also defended his department's treatment of us that night, saying we were as much to blame for the seven hours of questioning as anyone. He said we never did account for twenty minutes of our time between leaving home and reaching the American Legion. And he was puzzled that, in spite of George being a construction worker and handling fish at a bass tournament, his hands were "surgically clean."

George and I had a good laugh over that one. I distinctly remember telling the interrogating officer exactly how that twenty minutes was spent. We stopped at Poor Jim's to wait for Stephen and Mary. I helped Mary clear tables. The men sat outside and had a cigarette.

And George wasn't a construction worker either. He was a painter. Unlike the occasional painter who uses paint thinner on his hands, George used a special cleansing lotion with lanolin that cut any kind of paint quickly and left his hands soft and smooth. He didn't handle fish that day either. He helped with the boats.

From Ray's attorney, Darrell Deputy: "I got the impression that Billy received a vicarious thrill from the shootings. Once he started, he just kept going."

Deputy said he did not dispute Ray's involvement in the homicides. "As you look back on it, Ray Richardson was a young man that was subject to being influenced by his accomplice. He was easily led down the road."

The article mentioned that Ray was believed to be living near his grandparents in Arizona. This news unsettled us deeply. Why did he have to pick on our West? We gave him Missouri.

From the Prosecutor: "The two little girls, the two young men—what would they be doing today? I'd like to see them today. I'd like to introduce them to my children. I feel a loss. I regret that they aren't able to be around and be with us."

We didn't know it then, but this big anniversary spread would do us a great service in the very near future.

* * *

Less than four months later, we received a letter in the mail from the Board of Probation and Parole. Billy Dyer was scheduled for a parole consideration hearing on February 9, 1988. As parents of the victims, we had the right to attend the hearing and present our views. If we did not wish to attend, we were welcome to express our opinion by letter.

I reread the letter over and over again. I had been told Billy might have a parole hearing in ten months, and had been preparing myself emotionally and spiritually for the occasion. But this was too early, and I wasn't fully prepared.

I'd been trying to deal with my stand on forgiveness for quite a while now. While on a speaking engagement in Texas to talk to a group on grief recovery, I met a man named Tim Culver who had spent twelve years in prison on drug charges. He was not scheduled to be the speaker that evening, but the scheduled speaker's plane never arrived, so Tim was asked to fill in.

He told a story of dealing and manufacturing drugs, of selling drugs to his own sister, who overdosed and died. He told of guilt and agony, grief and pain; of urinating blood and nearly dying in his cell; of crying out to God and finding forgiveness in Christ. He worked for Prison Ministries in Texas now, devoting his life to reaching out to others like himself.

"Only two percent of the prisoners we talk to will honestly be converted for Christ," he admitted. "But of that two percent, ninety-eight percent will never return to prison. The conversion will be lasting, and we will have made a difference."

Throughout his speech, several people in the audience looked back at me, wondering how I was taking his story. I hung on every word and cried inside.

Afterward I came to him and held out my arms. "Brother?" I whispered.

He hugged me, and the tears came for both of us. "You helped me so much today, Tim," I confessed. "You represent the criminal to me. It was a side I needed to understand. You gave me hope for Billy and Ray."

"You've helped me, too," he said. "You represent the victim that I hurt with my crimes. You helped me to see the other side. Would you be willing to do an interview with me about victims and forgiveness?"

We met in the lodge that evening after the last speaker was finished and the guests had retired to their cabins. We talked for three hours into the morning, understanding what each of us represented, and how, through Christ, we could love one other and forgive.

I asked Tim to help me reach Billy to try to find out how he was doing, and if he even sought forgiveness for his crime. I knew a parole hearing was coming, and I needed to know if Billy was sorry for what he'd done. Had he found Christ and changed like Tim had? Tim promised to write to the prison chaplain to ask him to visit with Billy. But the chaplain was old and unpaid, and when Billy refused to talk with him, he would not pursue it. We had come up empty.

Now I held a letter from the parole board, announcing a hearing ten months earlier than I expected, and I didn't quite know where I stood because I didn't know how Billy felt.

"It's rather late in the ball game to finally be asking me what I think they should do with him," George replied. "Why didn't they consult me about the sentencing in the first place?"

George had absolutely no desire whatsoever to attend the parole hearing. He didn't even want to bother with sending a letter.

"They won't listen to what we have to say anyway," he snapped. "If they intend to release the little S.O.B., they'll do it no matter what we say. I resent all the attention Billy's getting from all the publicity. He thrives on it."

But for me, a letter wasn't nearly enough. I wanted to go to the parole hearing and see for myself. Most states didn't even have laws to allow victims a voice in the matter. Missouri had only passed the law less than a year before, which was why we never had a chance to speak before Ray's release in 1984. I wanted to go to the prison and attend the hearing, and I would not be persuaded otherwise.

"We have a right to be there, George," I argued. "For once somebody is asking me what I think about what happened. It's my duty as a victim to go–if only to set a precedent. To say, yes, I want the right to know what's going on and have a voice in the matter. We either use it or lose it."

But George knew that wasn't my main purpose for going. He knew I needed to reconcile in my own heart whether Billy was sorry for what he did, just in case they did release him. It was something I had needed to do with Ray and was never given the chance. The fear of not knowing kept our lives in chains.

I called my dad and asked him to buy me a plane ticket to St. Louis for February 6. My sister Dawn agreed to drive me down to Jefferson City for the hearing.

I still had a few weeks to get ready, and I prayed constantly that God would guide me and give me wisdom. Meanwhile, Dawn put out the word to all family members to write to the parole board to fight Billy's release. She called the *Springfield News-Leader* and asked for an interview and an article on the parole hearing.

On January 27, the *News-Leader* ran an article by Connie Farrow, and the heading jumped off the page: "Killer of 4 Children to Be Considered for Parole."

"We don't feel that he, or anybody for that matter who commits a crime like that, deserves to be released after serving only eleven years," Dawn was quoted in the article. "The family is outraged that he is even being considered for parole."

She urged everyone who felt strongly about it to write to the parole board and protest Billy's release.

The newspaper sent a reporter to the prison to interview Bill Duncan, a member of the Board of Probation and Parole. I think the interview may have sobered the board to think clearly about their responsibility to the community. This hearing would not go unnoticed.

Duncan said he would not speculate on Billy Dyer's chances of being released, but he did say most inmates serve an average of fifteen years on such charges.

"I can't predict what the board will do as far as his release is concerned, and it wouldn't be fair for me to say," said Duncan. "I will say that this is a very conservative board. We take a number of items into account before we release someone back into society."

He said the board would consider among other things: the seriousness of the crime; the amount of time served; Billy's criminal past; his adjustment in prison; and the concerns of the victims and the community.

According to board policy, an inmate serving a life sentence for first-degree murder received before 1984 may be considered for parole every two years if he wishes. Duncan mentioned Billy Dyer was reviewed in 1982 and 1986, and was denied parole both times. He wasn't allowed to say why the inmate was denied parole.

This was news to us. It was sobering to think this was already Billy's third parole consideration. His chances of release seemed greater the third time around, and that feeling of betrayal returned at not being told. If they let him out before I knew if he had changed, I wouldn't sleep at night wondering if he was out there.

They interviewed the prison warden that day, too. Bill Armontrout said Billy was being housed in protective custody and did not work in the prison system.

"An inmate is placed in protective custody when he has enemies in the prison system. That doesn't mean he necessarily has done anything wrong. Sometimes it's for their own safety."

Neither the parole board nor the warden would comment on Billy's adjustment to prison life. We didn't know if he was a troublemaker or a peacemaker.

But the article served to stir the public and caused enough stink in the community to be considered an issue. I received a call from the prison warden at Dawn's house the evening before the hearing. Billy had waived his right to his parole hearing and was asking that it be set back until September 1989. I had come fifteen hundred miles for nothing.

* * *

The news that Billy was waiving his parole hearing left me even more puzzled than before. Did he waive the hearing because he felt he hadn't served his time? Or because he'd heard I would be there and feared my presence at the hearing? Whatever his reason, his waiver deprived me of the chance to find out how he was and if he was sorry, and, therefore worthy of being forgiven.

Not knowing was chewing at me from the inside out. I had traveled too far not to find out. So I called the prison and talked to the warden's secretary, requesting permission to visit Billy.

"Are you on his visitor's list?" a middle-aged woman's voice inquired.

"No, ma'am," I said. "I've never visited him before."

"Are you a relative?" she asked.

"No. No, I'm not."

"Then how are you connected with this inmate?"

"He murdered my children ten years ago."

There was an awkward silence on the other end. I drew a deep breath and continued.

"I've been trying to find out how he is," I explained. "I tried to reach him through the chaplain, but he refused to talk to him. I've traveled fifteen hundred miles in hopes of talking to him. But he waived his parole hearing today and that took away my chance to see him face-to-face. If I could just see him, make eye contact with him..."

Her voice sparked with skepticism. "I think I understand how you feel."

"No, you don't know," I cried. "I'm sorry. But you don't know. Nobody knows how I feel except me and God. I need to see him, to tell him that I forgive him, and that I hate what he did, but I don't hate him."

There was another silent pause.

"You do understand that we have strict guidelines for visitations," she said in a pert, business-like voice. "The inmate will have to agree to a visit, and the warden will have to approve it. He's on another line right now. I will have him call you when he gets off the phone."

"Thank you," I said, and hung up the phone. I turned to Dawn, who had been straining to keep up with the conversation. "I may get to see him. I have to pray."

I went into Dawn's bedroom and knelt in the darkness, willing God to come to me as He had back in that dark motel room years before.

"Dear Heavenly Father," I prayed. "I've come so far. You know what's in my heart. If we reach Billy, he'll never kill again. Don't let Satan win. Please soften Billy's and the warden's hearts. If it be Your will, Father, please help me get through to Billy. Help me with the right words to say to the warden, to make him understand why I need to see him. Put the words into my mouth."

The phone rang down the hallway.

"In Jesus' name, Amen." I rose from the darkness to meet the call.

"It's the warden," Dawn said as she handed me the phone. I took it pensively.

"Yes, sir."

"This is Warden Armontrout," a husky voice replied. "I understand you wish to visit with an inmate."

"Warden Armontrout," I stumbled, not knowing what title was appropriate. "Ten years ago, I knew a fourteen-year-old boy who needed someone to care. And I cared. He ate my food. He slept in my house. He played with my kids. I took him to the movies...and he returned my kindness by killing my children.

"Nobody's ever told me why he did it. I still care very much about Billy, and I wonder how he's doing, how he's grown up. I didn't always feel this way. It's been a long battle. But I'm a Christian now, and I want him to know that I forgive him for what he did. The Bible says we should love the sinner and hate the sin. And I do. I don't hate Billy, and I want to tell him. I have some books I want to give him that may help."

The warden remained silent and waited for me to continue.

"If Billy's sitting in that cell feeling he's totally worthless, nobody can love him, and God can't forgive him; if I can walk in that prison and tell him I forgive him and God loves him, then maybe he'll realize he's worth something. So someday when he gets out...and he will get out someday...then he won't hurt anybody again. I don't want any more mothers going through what I went through. I just want to try to reach him, so I can go home and know I tried."

The warden sighed. The tone of his voice made it unclear whether he believed my story. "You do understand that you will be thoroughly searched. Metal detectors will be used on you and everything you carry in."

"I understand that," I replied.

"Okay, you come tomorrow at nine o'clock. We'll do our best to get you in to see him. But he'll have to agree to the visit."

"Thank you," I cried, both nervous and excited at the same time. "Thank you so much."

"You understand there will be bars between you and Bill. You won't be allowed to touch him."

"That's fine. Great," I answered him hastily. "I promise you, I mean him no harm. The bars are fine. It protects me, too. I won't be wearing anything I shouldn't." Then I remembered the metal belt buckle on the dress I planned to wear.

"The metal detectors will catch it," the warden assured me.

"Thanks so much, Warden Armontrout. And I'd appreciate it if, when you talk to Billy, you relay how I feel. Maybe he'll agree to see me then."

"Come tomorrow," he said again and hung up the phone. I returned the receiver to its cradle and lifted my eyes to heaven in thanks.

That evening, after Dawn put her kids to bed, we talked about what to expect tomorrow and how much I wanted to find Billy changed. I had planned to give Billy a nice hardbound Bible, but replaced it with a soft cover one after Tim told me that hardbound books are often not allowed in prison. I took great care to mark a number of scriptures in yellow that talked about God's ability to forgive. Inside the front cover I mentioned there were special messages for him and listed the page numbers.

At Matthew 5:44, I highlighted, "Love your enemies, bless them that curse you, do good to them that hate you, and pray for them which despitefully use you, and persecute you." In the margin I added, "Billy, I forgive you."

At Luke 23:34, I wrote "Jesus forgave His own murderers." At Luke 15:4-7, the story of the Lost Sheep, I added, "Billy, you are that one sheep." At John 15:10-14, I said, "Jesus laid down His life for you."

And at Psalm 51, where David acknowledges his sins and prays to be released from his transgressions, I pleaded, "I hope this will become your prayer. David was also a murderer." At 1 John 1:9, "If we confess our sins, he is faithful and just to forgive our sins, and to cleanse us from all unrighteousness." I wrote simply, "Will you, Billy?"

I wanted so much to reach him. I had several other little books I wanted to give him about prisoners who had found Christ. I had just finished writing a topical book on grief recovery entitled *Good-byes Are Not Forever*. One full chapter was devoted to learning to forgive. It was in the publisher's hands, but it wasn't yet published, so I had a copy made of just that one chapter to give to Billy, to show him how I really felt about forgiveness.

Dawn listened as I explained to her the reason I wanted to give Billy each individual book. She stayed calm and even enthusiastic for quite a while, and then the tears broke through.

"Joy, I've been trying so hard to support you on this," she shook her head, "but I really don't understand what you're doing. I know I understand more than the rest of the family because I've found Christ, too. But I'm sorry. I can't forgive Billy and Ray for what they did. I hate them! And the hate is so intense! I want to kill them for what they took from us. How can you find a way to forgive them?"

The tears came for me, too, emotional tears from deep within.

"Dawn, I hate what they did, too. They killed my family! They altered my life irreparably forever! And God hates what they did. But God is willing to forgive them if they repent. If they are truly sorry and turn away from their sins, God can forgive them. And Billy and Ray will have just as much right to the Kingdom as my children."

Dawn looked up at me. "But how do you live with that? Knowing they can have the same reward as the kids? They're the enemy!"

"The Bible tells me to love my enemy. To pray for those who hurt me. To forgive seventy times seven. And it's hard. And I fight it inside all the time because I don't even understand how I can forgive.

"It's a day-by-day decision, and some days are really hard. All I can say is, I can't hate them. I abhor what they did, but I just can't hate them. And the only way I can explain it is it's Christ working in me. I couldn't do it otherwise."

Chapter 21

One Hour In Prison

Dawn searched for another radio station to replace the one we'd lost. It was the third one already since leaving St. Louis early that morning. With seventy-five miles behind us, another fifty still lay ahead, but the roads were clear, and we'd left in plenty of time to get there.

Following the beat of the music, she tapped her fingers against the steering wheel. She knew it was an odd emotion for someone going to a prison to see a murderer, but she was giddy with excitement. After all these years of being tossed aside by both the system and the family, she was getting to play an active role.

There never seemed to be enough room for her before, in the trials or the grieving. There was always someone else making the decisions, and always someone else who needed comforting more. She'd been expected to sit on the sidelines like a good little girl and keep quiet, and she'd done that well.

Nobody seemed to notice she needed comforting, too. She lived with the same fear for her three children that George and I lived with ours–a prison of fear that kept her from enjoying the kind of carefree social life so many of her friends enjoyed. It was a prison she couldn't even hope to be paroled from. How could they even consider letting the killer out of his?

This trip was like a gift to her. At last, she felt like her feelings mattered, too. Although it hadn't been promised yet, she hoped to convince the warden to let her come in with me. She had never met Billy, only heard stories about him. She wondered what this insensitive killer looked like, what he would say to us after all the damage he caused our family.

If he thought all of the victims died that night he was wrong. That one half hour of his life ruined the lives of everyone who loved the children. One half hour wiped out the happiness, the security, the wholeness of an entire family. She was a part of that family. She was a victim, too. She felt she deserved to finally confront the one who caused it all.

She didn't know yet what she would say to him. There were so many questions. So much anger inside. But with me there, actually willing to forgive him and tell him about Jesus, she hadn't decided just how she would go about letting Billy know how she felt about him.

She had decided to just take it as it came, listen to what I said, and see how Billy reacted. She would go in with an open mind. But she was worried about me, worried that all this Prison Ministries influence might cloud my judgment, might make me see something in Billy that wasn't really there.

She could act as the balancing rod. Between my hopes and her skepticism, she hoped we could come to a realistic conclusion about Billy's true character. But more than anything, she just needed to be there.

We rolled into Jefferson City an hour early for our appointment. The drizzling rain and the drab appearance of the town did nothing to repress our enthusiasm for the adventure that lay ahead. Dawn suggested we find a place to have breakfast and wind down before heading over to the prison.

We located the prison on the map the warden sent me with the parole hearing notice and satisfied ourselves that we would have no trouble finding it. Then we drove through the center of town and out both highways in search of a fast-food place for a quick bite to eat.

To our amazement, we couldn't find even one. So we went into a restaurant inside a downtown hotel, quite elegant really. We ordered fruited yogurt and bagels with cream cheese, which was totally out of character for us. We chatted like two proper ladies out for tea until it was time to head for the prison.

* * *

Even from a block away, the prison was a sobering sight as we pulled into a parking place and climbed out of the car. The sky was dreary and spat rain at us. We left our coats behind, leaving one less thing to be scanned at the door, and shivered against the chill wind as we made our way down the inclined road that led to the prison.

As we drew closer, I gazed over the high brick wall, topped with loops of nasty-looking razor wire, to catch a glimpse of the prison beyond. The prison was constructed of pitted red bricks, an ancient fortress of a building with tiny windows spattered across the sides.

A small balcony clung to one side, fully fenced in with wire and bars. An exercise area for the most dangerous criminals, I guessed, or the ones under protective custody like Ray had been his whole time here. And like Billy was now. I tried to imagine him inside the tiny cage dangling high above the ground. What could he do in there? What could he see?

The prison yard afforded no inspiring view of the outside world. No hills. No mountains. No woods. It wasn't anything like the prisons in Colorado, which were so new and had such beautiful views of the mountains surrounding them.

What a morbid existence, I thought, to be locked up and not be able to even look out and see a mountain, a hill or a forest. I had once cried that prisoners had more luxury than some families; with pool tables, television, exercise equipment and live music shows. But as I looked across the compound, I couldn't think of one thing they could have done to make this place look more dreary. If Billy was going to murder, he should have done it in a state with a nicer prison.

We crossed the street to the north side of the prison. The massive wall cast a shadow on the cracked sidewalk below, keeping the ice from melting and making our walk hazardous at best. We rounded the corner to the front of the building.

On the other side of a tall nine-foot gate, inmates dressed in blue jumpsuits unloaded boxes from the back of a bus. They shuffled along awkwardly, their ankles in chains.

Dawn shook her head. "How do they work that way?" she said. "I'd fall on my face if I had to walk like that."

Did I detect pity in her voice? One of the inmates looked our way and whistled. We hurried on to the double doors.

A dozen people, all women and children, were already waiting to be signed in. Two young black women with four small children in tow meekly answered questions as the female guard scanned them with a metal detector. One of them reached into her purse and pulled out a stack of photographs she wished to take in with her.

"These were taken at his son's birthday party," she explained to the guard. "And this is a picture the littlest one drew for his daddy."

The guard examined the items without a word. The young mother just stood there, embarrassed by the silence. If the guard were human, I thought, she'd bend down and ask the little boy how old he was. She'd compliment the little one on his drawing and tell him how much his daddy was going to love it.

The busty, overstuffed woman at the desk was even less human than the guard. I watched her with all the others. Her snippy attitude made everyone she encountered here feel like a criminal, and I rather resented her for it. These people here had broken no laws. They were only visiting those who had. There was no crime in that. I hated the way she belittled the families, especially the children.

Our turn finally came at the desk. The woman looked up at us without a smile. I'd made up my mind that I did not want to deal with her.

"My name is Joy Swift," I said. "I'd like to speak with Warden Armontrout." I handed her my driver's license for identification the way I'd seen the others do. She glanced at it and shoved it back to me.

"What is this pertaining to?" she demanded.

"I spoke with him on the phone yesterday about seeing an inmate...William Patrick Dyer."

She opened the filing cabinet, retrieved Billy's file and scanned its contents. "Your name is not on his visitor's file. Are you related to Mr. Dyer?"

"In a way," I blurted. "He murdered my children."

Her eyes got big, and every eye in the room singled me out. I looked over at Dawn for strength. "Look, can I just see Warden Armontrout? He knows why I'm here."

The woman let out an impatient huff and picked up the phone.

A few minutes later a man appeared wearing an important- looking uniform. He looked much kinder than the overstuffed woman at the desk.

"Are you Warden Armontrout?" I asked.

"No, I'm Assistant Warden Newby. Let's go out here so we can talk."

We followed him out to the foyer. He made sure the door closed completely before he spoke.

"Bill Dyer has agreed to see you. You'll be allowed one hour to visit with him."

My heart began to race as soon as he said it. But why he did he call him Bill? I could never call him anything but Billy.

"That's great," I said. "An hour is plenty."

"The warden won't allow a contact visit. Bill will be in a glass booth. You'll use a telephone to talk to him. And a guard will be watching the whole time."

"That's fine," I replied. "I didn't need to touch him anyway. Is there any chance my sister can come in with me? For moral support?"

Newby shook his head. "I'm afraid the warden wouldn't allow that."

Dawn's face fell. Again, she was left out. I felt so sorry for her.

"It's okay," she said, visibly disappointed. Happy for me, and jealous at the same time, because I was going in and she was not. "I'll just drive around town for an hour and be back. Here's the books you wanted to give him." She handed the sack of books to me.

"Those will have to be left at the desk," Newby reminded me. "We'll take them downstairs and have them scanned before he can have them."

Dawn watched as I was scanned with the metal detector and made it through the first of three security gates that would take me to the visitation room. I waved good-bye to her through the glass as I stood before the second one.

"Place your hand over the light," the guard in the glass booth called. I didn't understand him. He acted put out and repeated the instructions.

"Well, excuse me," I thought to myself. "I don't do this every day. How am I supposed to know how to open it?" Instead I smiled sweetly and moved on through to the third gate.

I stepped into the visitation room in time to see three inmates enter through an interior door. They all wore the same thing: light gray shirt, dark slacks and white terrycloth slippers. The young black woman and her children rushed to greet one of them. Other inmates and their families were gathered in padded chairs or around big tables chatting happily, sharing stories, holding hands.

A large glassed-in booth protruded into the room. Divided in half by a partition, it had six phones on each side. Two guards mingled about the room, with a third one inside the glass booth. The male guard came to me and led me over to the booth.

"When he comes out, you'll sit here," he said, pointing to the last stool on that side. He picked up the receiver hanging on the side. "This works just like a regular telephone. But it will be a few minutes before they bring him up. Why don't you sit over at that table until he comes."

I thanked him and took a seat at the big round table. The door inside the booth opened, and two inmates were escorted in. The guard shouted through the glass to the man inside.

"Take them to the other side. This side is reserved. He's coming out."

The guard inside the booth quickly moved the inmates over to the other side. The door opened again, and the guard barked the same command. "Take them to the other side. He's coming out."

He never said Billy's name. He just kept calling him "he." Both of the guards seemed terribly nervous about the situation. I could feel the woman guard's eyes on my back, but every time I turned to look at her, she quickly turned the other way.

The male guard kept looking at me and shaking his head. Finally, he came over and sat down across the table. He started to talk, but the words were caught by the lump in his throat.

I smiled up at him. "This is hard," I said.

He looked up at the ceiling, searching his mind for the right words to say. His eyes met mine.

"You know, none of us can understand what you're doing here. How you can see him after..." The lump in his throat caught again and he couldn't finish.

I nodded to let him know I sympathized. "I don't really understand it either. I never thought I'd have the strength to come here. But it's something I need to do."

The door inside the booth opened again and the guard stood clear to allow the inmate to enter. It was Billy. He was taller now. Definitely older. His hair style hadn't changed much, but a full mustache set off his thick dark eyebrows. I made a mental note to remember to look at his fingertip, the one he'd shot off when he killed the kids.

The guard motioned for Billy to take the stool at the end of the booth. I took my place on the other side and picked up the phone.

"Hi, Billy," I said, as if we were old friends meeting after a long absence.

Billy smiled that same fourteen-year-old smile he used to when he'd come over to play. Innocent, and yet villainous at the same time. He was the only one I knew who could smile like that. And there was that glint in his eyes he reserved just for me.

"Hi," he answered back.

We both laughed nervously. Billy leaned against the counter to get closer to the glass.

"You know, when the warden told me you wanted to see me I got kind of nervous. I've been pacing downstairs for an hour, wondering what to say."

I shot him a knowing glance. "I know that feeling. I did my pacing last night. Did the warden tell you why I wanted to see you?"

"No. He just told me you wanted to come talk to me. I knew you were in town for the parole hearing from the newspaper. I figured after you took the time to come here, I owed it to you to see you whether you wanted to yell at me or whatever."

"Well, I didn't come to yell at you," I assured him. "I came to find out how you are. I was hoping to find out at the parole hearing. Then when you waived the hearing, I thought, I didn't come all this way not to find out."

"So what do you want to know?" Billy asked.

"Billy, I need to know if you've changed. I need to know that when you walk out of this prison you're not going hurt anybody again. All the relatives are protesting your release. But I don't know how I stand on you getting out of here until I know whether you've changed."

Billy shrugged.

"So, why did you waive the parole hearing?"

"I just didn't realize there were so many people that still wanted me in." Billy said. "When that newspaper article came out, I figured the board wouldn't look at my work record or my institutional record and give me a fair hearing. I just figured it was best to wait. I'll go again in September of next year."

I hid my relief. At least that was another year I didn't have to worry about. A whole year to get my feelings together.

"So, what's it like in here?" I asked.

Billy pushed his lip out. "It's okay. It's a pretty decent prison."

"Are you still in solitary?"

"What do you mean by solitary?" Billy challenged.

"I don't know. By yourself, I guess."

"I'm in what they call Ward J," he explained. "It's where they put those who steal from other inmates or have enemies in the system. But I'm busy most of the time. Contrary to that newspaper article, I have two jobs."

"Oh really," I tried to sound impressed. "What do you do?"

"I work in the metal shop during the day and in the kitchen in the evenings. I'm thinking about giving up the kitchen job, though. It's better to keep busy in here. But two jobs keep me too busy."

There was an awkward pause. I changed the subject.

"Billy, I just want you to know there isn't a day that goes by that I don't think about the kids, wondering how much they'd have grown by now. Seeing you makes me realize how grown up the boys would be. How much I miss having them here."

He pursed his lips and looked at me sympathetically.

"This is going to sound strange, Billy," I said. "But there are times when I even miss you because you were a part of my life back when the kids were alive. The day they were killed, I never saw you again, either."

Billy nodded, his mouth tight.

"I used to wonder," I continued, "if you ever wanted to tell me something. But there was no way for me to get to you. I don't think the police would have liked it if I came asking to see you at the jail."

"Yeah," Billy said. "I thought about that, too."

"Billy, I have one question that's been eating at me for years."

"Go ahead and ask," he said.

"Why, Billy? Why did you do it?"

Billy looked serious for a moment and then turned his gaze to the ceiling. "I don't know. I've had psychologists asking me that for ten years, and I don't know why I did it."

"Well, did we ever do anything to make you mad? To make you want to hurt us?"

"No. You were always nice to me," he said, then a puzzled look crossed his brow. "I don't know why I did it. In a way I think it's good that I got caught. If I'd have gotten away with that there's no telling what all I'd have done."

"So did Ray do any of the killing?"

"No," he shook his head. "I killed them all. The only reason I took Ray with me was because I needed him to show me how to reload the gun. I didn't know how."

"They didn't tell me when Ray was paroled. I learned about it a year after he got out. I'll probably never know how he is."

Billy leaned closer. "Well, you see, they just passed this law letting victims know last year. When they let Ray out they didn't have to tell you."

"I know. I don't think that's fair. I think we should have the right to know. I didn't know until a few days ago that you've already had two hearings."

Billy nodded. "They've been doing a lot of new things. They're letting victims talk to their assailants now, and I think that's good. It helps them to better understand the impact of what they did."

Another awkward silence. It was time to tell him how I really felt.

"Billy, I came here to forgive you," I said, "if you're sorry for what you did. I hate what you did to my kids. I'll always hate what you did. But I want you to know that I don't hate you. You have to understand that forgiveness did not come easily for me. It's taken a long time for me to reach this point, and I don't want you to take it lightly."

Billy nodded again, but said nothing.

"I brought you some books to help you better understand what I'm trying to say to you. I wanted to give them to you personally, but the warden says they have to be searched and scanned and all that."

"They're pretty thorough here," Billy said.

"Like I hid a bomb in one of them," I joked. "You should have seen the looks I got when I came here. Especially that lady at the front desk! Nobody understands why I wanted to see you. This is simply not done!"

Billy tapped the glass with his knuckle. "I don't know why they felt this booth was necessary."

"I don't know either," I shrugged. "They're just being careful."

"Yeah," Billy said. "They're good at that."

"I don't know if you already have one, Billy, but one of the books I'm giving you is a Bible. I marked some verses I want you to read, so you'll understand what I'm trying to say about forgiveness. And then there's some other little books on Prison Ministries. I hope you'll read them."

"I will," he promised. "I'll read it all. I've taken some Bible studies with several different denominations. I've been writing to this lady in Illinois, and she's sent me some really good books."

"That's good," I encouraged him. "Keep it up. I'm proud of you."

"So how's George?" Billy asked.

I gave him a stern glance. "George was not at all happy about my coming here. He isn't anywhere near to forgiving you. He feels that forgiving you is like saying it was all right what you did. And, Billy, it's not." I looked him straight in the eye.

"You could have taken anything else we owned, and we would have recovered. But not the kids. George feels like I betrayed him by coming here. Coming here was probably worse than committing adultery because I am consorting with the enemy."

"I'm sorry," Billy said. "I didn't want to cause you two any more hurt."

"Hey, well. This was something I needed to do for my own healing," I explained. "You didn't make me come. It's taken me a long time, but I'm finally able to separate the sin from the sinner. George may reach that point someday. Then again he may not."

"I can understand that," Billy said.

"Billy, if you want to separate yourself from the sin, then I have to forgive you. That's what God wants me to do."

I smiled at him and tried to add some humor to lighten the tension.

"I've been busting my tail trying to find out how you are. I've been in contact with a guy from Prison Ministries and everything else to try to get to you. We even tried to send the chaplain to talk to you. We just kept coming up empty."

Billy perked up. "I watched this prison ministries film in the rec room one day and it had a guy...oh, what was that guy's name?...from the Charles Manson family."

"It was Tex Watson," I told him.

"Yeah. That's the one. He was converted to Christ and wanted to tell the families he was sorry. It was a good film."

I was dumbfounded. "Billy, I saw that film at my church. You won't believe this, but the day I saw that film was the day I started to forgive you."

Billy's eyes got big. "Wow. It's a small world."

He didn't know it, but the Illinois woman he'd been corresponding with by mail for the last year was someone I'd asked to look him up. Cladie was in Prison Ministries in Illinois when I met her at a speaking engagement in June of 1987. She'd used an inmate to get her address to Billy. Billy wrote to her asking for any Bible studies she might have available to inmates.

Cladie responded without mentioning my name, to give Billy a chance to reveal himself as he saw fit. She sent him numerous books, tapes and Bible studies. Her letters always encouraged Billy to be the best he could be. "An idle mind is the devil's workshop," she admonished.

Billy wrote to her in a relaxed way. He seemed to be sincerely searching for Bible answers and it was clear by his questions that he was reading the materials she sent him. But he never knew I was behind it all. He would probably put the connection together when he got the books I brought. On the back cover of one of the books was Cladie's address. She was the one who gave it to me.

The hour was getting long. But I wasn't about to give up even a minute of it. I would probably never be able to come here again.

"So do your parents ever come to see you?" I asked.

Billy looked sad. "Ron and Mom moved back to Connecticut. Ron's a truck driver, so they're on the road for weeks at a time. They come to see me about once a year. But they won't ever talk about what happened."

"That's too bad."

His eyes got bright again. "I've put in for a transfer to the Connecticut prison. They have a real good optometry program up there that would teach me how to grind glasses. I've also considered getting a B.A. in sociology to figure out why I did what I did."

I fought back my jealousy. My children would never go to college, never learn a trade. My kids were dead. I slapped the feeling away.

"That would be nice to get back near family," I agreed. "I want you to do whatever you can to make something of yourself. I mean that. Because someday they're going to let you out of here, no matter how I feel, and I have to know that you're not the same boy that came here. I have to know you're never going to hurt anybody again."

"I understand that," he nodded.

The guard tapped my shoulder. "I'm sorry. Your time is up."

I thanked him and turned back to Billy. "Well, that's it, I guess. Thank you for seeing me."

"Hey, anytime you want to come, I'll okay it," Billy promised. "And if George wants to come, even if he wants to just chew me out, that's okay. The front desk can give you my address if you want to write."

"I'll be sure and get it," I said. "And if you ever want to get hold of me, write to me through my publisher. I wrote the address inside the cover of one of the books. George would be really upset if a letter from you came in the mail."

"I understand," Billy smiled again.

"You take care, Billy, and you work to be the best you can be. I mean it because I do still care."

Billy nodded and hung up the phone. He glanced back at me one last time before he disappeared. The guard escorted me to the door, and I left through the three gates.

He certainly hadn't wasted his mind while here, I thought, as I passed through to the other side. He's very intelligent. He could go a long way if he focused on being good. His finger! I forgot to look at his finger. Suddenly I could think of a hundred things I forgot to ask him.

Dawn was waiting for me in the entry. I rushed her out the door.

"So how did it go?" she asked anxiously.

"Good. It went good."

"I found a Hardee's out on the highway. Let's go get some lunch and you can tell me all about it."

I did my best to fill her in over roast beef sandwiches. But my brain buzzed from the experience.

"I wish you were a camcorder," she said, "so I could rewind you and play you back. I want everything down to the last detail."

"I know. I wish you could have been there. I know I needed to do this. But so did you."

"I'm used to it by now," she said with a shrug. "I walked around the state capital while you were in there. I had to park three blocks away. And then when I got there, the people in the halls all looked at me like I didn't belong. It made me feel second class, kind of non-person, and the government didn't understand how I felt and didn't care to. It all seemed fitting. That's the way I felt today."

"I'm sorry."

"So, do you think he's changed?"

"I don't know. He said he's in a Ward J for troublemakers, but he didn't say what he'd done to win that cell assignment. He never did tell me he was sorry. But he's definitely studied the Bible with several groups. Oddly, it's the same groups I've studied with. He'd even seen that film about Tex Watson."

"That's weird," Dawn said.

"I want to stop by the church here in town before we leave and see if the pastor will go see him. I think Billy's on the right track. But I also think he has a ways to go, and he has a better chance of getting there if he stays in. I don't want him out yet."

Chapter 22

It's Up to Billy

George and the kids met me at the airport the next day. I'd flown out several times before for speaking engagements, and always came home to big hugs and kisses. The kids rushed to meet me. But George was sullen and would not come near to give me a hug. I showered my attention on the children and let him hurt.

Seeing Billy was betrayal. I had taken his side, told him what he'd done was forgiven. It was unforgivable and rocked our marriage more than anything either of us had ever done. I avoided him for a week.

Finally, I confronted him, and his anger poured out in hot tears. His hurt was so deep it made me cry. But going to the prison was something I needed to do for my own healing. I would not apologize for it. Not after I'd been denied so many things in the past. I only apologized that I hurt George so much in the process.

We cried together, talked it out, and moved ahead. After all we'd been through together, we couldn't allow this to tear our marriage apart. But I wasn't through being concerned about Billy, and I never would be as long as he lived.

For George's sake, any connection with Billy from here on out would have to be done behind his back. I hated it that way, but it was the only way to allow me to do what I needed to do and still protect George from the hurt. I respected that he needed to wipe his hands of any connection with the killer of his children. It was a matter of loyalties to him, and he remained loyal to the kids.

I only wished he could respect that I was playing by a different set of rules. I had to satisfy my own need to know if Billy had changed.

Connie Farrow received a letter from Billy the day of the foiled parole hearing to let her know of his disappointment about the newspaper article that ran prior to that date. He enclosed a copy of the letter he sent to the parole board, "so that you would have a clear understanding of why I am refusing my parole hearing...

"I am under the impression that the administration only releases information that is negative or non-committal," he wrote. "In support of my statement concerning the administration's statements about my case; they informed you that I have not worked since my incarceration when in fact I have been working at the prison's metal plant for the past three years, with the exception of five months, and have received good work reports from my civilian foreman."

He invited Connie to contact him if she had any questions. Connie wrote to ask if he'd be interested in doing an interview to tell his side of the story. Billy agreed. The result was a two-page spread in the Sunday edition.

The article was confusing to me. The full-length picture Billy posed for depicted just the look he wanted. His arms were crossed boldly against his lanky frame as he leaned against the cell wall. A curl of black hair fell across his forehead, and that dark mustache added to the dastardly look he seemed to be trying so hard to portray. His eyes, if anything, had grown deeper and more evil. That glint was gone. He cocked his right brow in defiance.

Most of the article that followed offered little new evidence. Yet his purpose for doing the interview wasn't fully clear, whether he was bragging about the killings, or justifying his actions to seek sympathy. I don't think Billy even knew. But the third paragraph was a grabber.

"Today he is 24 years old, hardened by his years behind bars, haunted by the bloody events that put him there—and for the first time, willing to speak about the crime that shocked and outraged Ozarkers more than a decade ago."

Billy was quoted as saying: "The way we talked about it...Ray and me...was that if they were there, we'd get one of the guns, shoot the people in the house, and take the rest of them."

Ray was promised a dinner at Billy's house for his help in the crime. Billy admitted his father never allowed guns in the house. He'd only shot a gun a few times before and knew very little about them.

"That was the reason I took Ray along. Because I didn't know how to load the gun."

His only explanation for singling out our family was that he knew George had a gun collection and that he, for a boy his age, "was overly interested in guns." Yet after obtaining two of them at a cost of four lives, he threw them both into the lake and never tried to recover them.

"That's why the crime is so totally senseless," Billy said almost laughing. "You know, at the time, it just doesn't enter your mind that they'll be the hottest thing in the state."

By his expression in the photo you could tell he honestly believed he was the hottest thing in the state. He admitted that the children didn't struggle and believed they would have let him take the guns.

He mentioned that he wanted to get a degree in sociology so he could understand, "why somebody does something like this." He blamed the killings on his parents' divorce; on being pulled away from his home in Connecticut and moving to a place he didn't feel comfortable in; on old Western movies where the outlaw showed no mercy and never left any witnesses to tell.

Billy admitted that getting caught was the last thing on his mind even though he'd bragged about his plan.

"Actually, in a way I think it's good that I got caught because if I could have gotten away with that, well, there's nothing I couldn't get away with."

He did say he was sorry now.

"There was a time when I wouldn't have admitted it for the world. I've had a long time to think about it. That's one thing this place does give you is time to think."

The reporter interviewed others in hopes of offering both sides of the story. Sheriff Whitten and Trooper Thomas said they had a hard time believing Dyer was sorry. Whitten revealed Billy's attempts to kill a guard and an inmate while in jail awaiting trial. Billy denied both incidents.

In regards to a motive, Whitten said, "Billy Dyer killed those kids because Billy Dyer wanted to kill those kids. I don't believe there's any other reason."

When asked if he thought he had served enough time, Billy said, "The way I look at that is that when they feel I've served my time, they'll let me go."

There was nothing in his interview that said, "I've changed. I'm a different man. I want to make it up to society somehow." Just, "When they feel I've served enough time, they'll let me go." Then what? The article left me very unsatisfied. I wondered if anything I'd said to him soaked in.

In a private phone conversation following the interview, Connie warned me to be careful.

"He's slick," she said. "Not only is he not sorry for what he did, he doesn't even fathom why he should be."

She confided also that the reason Billy was suspended from his prison job for five months was that he was caught plotting to escape, a detail somehow missing from his letter to Connie. I wondered how she was able to get so much information that I couldn't.

* * *

On February 28, 1988, Billy wrote to Cladie in Illinois and for the first time told her why he was sent to prison. He mentioned that he was visited by the mother of the children he had killed.

"I had no idea what to expect, and while I was waiting for them to set the visit up and call me up to the visiting room, a hundred different conversations were passing through my mind. When I went up there, she told me that she had no objections whatsoever to my being released as long as she could be certain that I could never do anything like that again.

"And then she forgave me for what I had done. That's what has really been on my mind: the courage it must have taken her to do that. I have read about forgiveness, but it has always seemed like an abstract theological idea. I don't know if that makes any sense or not; I've read about it, understood the doctrine, but have never actually seen it put into practice."

Cladie rejoiced at the letter. Billy still didn't know that Cladie knew me. But my visit evidently did make an impact on his mind.

On May 7, 1988, Billy wrote to me for the first time. My editor, Marvin Moore, read it to me over the phone.

"There's a lot I want to say and really don't know how to put it into words. When you were up here you said that you had no objections to my ever being released as long as you knew that I would never do something like that again.

"I know that you still feel anger at times. I also know that I am supposed to be here, and that's why it doesn't bother me to be locked up.

"You know that I go up before the parole board again in a year from September. If it will make you feel better I can just keep canceling the parole hearings indefinitely. Larry Whitten plans to contest the release, but I don't really care how he feels, especially since he seems to have treated everybody badly. But if it would bother you or George, I'd be more than happy to cancel the hearing when the time came."

Marvin wrote to Billy to let him know the letter arrived. He invited Billy to write if he had any questions about the Bible. Marvin was a former pastor.

Billy wrote again on December 28 and asked Marvin to read his letter to me over the phone. He also asked Marvin to help him understand.

"She forgave me for my crime, and although I can understand this on a spiritual level from my studies, I am having a hard time understanding how she could have overcome her human emotions to the point that would allow her to forgive me. It took a great deal of courage and faith for her to do that, and from talking to her on that day I know she meant it when she forgave me, it wasn't something she felt she had to do out of necessity for her beliefs."

Marvin called me while George was at work and read the letter to me.

"I have been continuing my studies of the Bible," Billy wrote. "One drawback that I think about a lot is that I am having a problem with God forgiving me for this. I know the Bible says that if we confess our sins, and are truly sorry for them, we will be forgiven; I also know that you forgave me, and were sincere when you did it.

"By the same token, Cain was forever banished for murdering Abel, and Judas was condemned for eternity for betraying Jesus. These were terrible acts, but I really committed an act that was as morally offensive as you can get. I hope I can understand this better as I get deeper into the Bible.

"As you know, I will be having a parole hearing in 9 months. If for any reason you feel that I should not go up but should set it back, just let me know and I'll do that. I mean for ANY reason. You have been through a lot over the past 11 years, and I don't want to cause you any more pain. If setting a hearing off for a couple of years will help, just let me know. I mean that."

Marvin wrote back and offered to send Billy a Today's English Version of the Bible for easier everyday reading. He also offered Billy the answers he needed to find peace within himself.

"In your letter you said that you have a hard time understanding how Joy could forgive you. You said that on a spiritual level, perhaps, you can understand her forgiveness, but on the human, emotional level it's hard to understand. I will respond to that question in two ways.

"First, from my conversations with Joy a couple of years ago when I first became acquainted with her, I know that she really did have a hard time with that. Forgiveness is not something that we humans, in our natural frame of mind, are able to do.

"Forgiveness is a gift from God. It is a change that God makes in our minds, because we cannot make it for ourselves. It is a miracle. So if it makes sense to you that God could work a miracle in Joy's mind that would make it possible for her to forgive you, then that's the explanation.

"Miracles like that often take time. God never forces us. He just keeps trying to influence us gently to let Him work those miracles in our minds. You've probably heard Christian people talk about 'conversion' and the 'new birth.' That's what they are talking about: the miracle that God works in our minds that makes it possible for us to forgive, to be kind even to our enemies, to love those who hate us or who have wronged us.

"In your letter you indicated that you are having quite a struggle with the idea that God can forgive you for the terrible crime you committed. I think I can understand how you feel. And the answer for you is the same as it was for Joy. Your ability to accept God's forgiveness has to be just as much a miracle as it was for Joy to grant forgiveness.

"On the rational, logical level we humans can often say, 'I know God has forgiven me because He said He would,' while on the emotional level we struggle with our feelings of not being forgiven. Sometimes God is able to work a miracle to help us forgive, or to feel forgiven, very quickly—almost in an instant. But I try not to insist that he always do it that way for me.

"When God works miracles in our minds He always takes into account our free wills, and our readiness for Him to do something for us. It took Joy time to grow to the point that she was able to forgive you, and maybe it will take a while for God to work a miracle in you that will help you to feel forgiven. Perhaps it would be better to say that God will help you to grow toward feeling forgiven than to think that it will happen all at once.

"You mentioned Cain and Judas. Yes, it's true that, so far as we know, they were not forgiven. I think the point is that they didn't ask for forgiveness. They didn't want forgiveness. There is no such thing as a sin in God's sight that is too morally offensive for Him to forgive, provided we sincerely want forgiveness and ask for it, and provided we confess the sin to Him and to the people we have wronged.

"That brings up one other thing I should mention about this matter of forgiveness, and learning to accept God's forgiveness. I know that when you and Joy talked, she told you that she forgave you. I don't know whether you told her that you realized how much you had hurt her and her family, how terribly you felt about it, and asked her to forgive you for what you did.

"If you did not do that, then you need to do it before you can feel God's forgiveness. Since you cannot talk to her in person at this point, you need to write her a letter. Address it to both her and George, and send it to me. That is one letter I think George should see, but I would let Joy decide how and when that should happen."

* * *

Billy wrote back two weeks later. It was addressed to George.

"I know that I have caused you a great deal of pain; more than you can probably ever forgive me for. I want you to know that I am very sorry for what I did to you and your children. I realize that 'sorry' isn't enough, and that your feelings about this are very deep. I feel that I've done more than just hurt people; I've scarred them forever, and that is something that will never heal.

"I don't want you to think that I am writing this letter as some type of parole board manipulation. I admit that I would like to get out someday, but if you feel that you would be offended by this in any way, just get word to me and I will simply close my parole file. I mean cancel it; period.

"I know that what I did was a terrible wrong, and unlike a lot of inmates, I understand that if I were to spend the rest of my life here it would be a token justice.

"I AM sorry for what I did to you, Joy, and your family. I will do anything to show you how sorry I am. I don't think there was a person around who knew any of us that was not hurt, and the fault is wholly mine. I know that there aren't any words I can say that will properly express this, or that can in any way alleviate your sense of loss and anger, but I needed to express my sorrow."

Marvin read the letter to me over the phone. I wanted George to hear it, but I knew he wasn't ready yet. His loyalty was still with the children.

I wrote back to Billy on February 20, 1989. Being Steve's birthday, I was particularly vulnerable to the grief I still carried. Birthdays were always rough—another year gone without the kids. It was a long letter, four pages in all.

"George and I did discuss your letter addressed to him, but he does not as yet want to hear it straight from you. He still feels that in forgiving you, he is saying that what you did was okay. And it is not.

"Your last letter indicated that you were seeking my opinion as to whether or not I want you paroled. I've been trying to determine how, as a Christian, I should deal with this issue. Unfortunately, my human nature tends to get in the way sometimes, and the pain you have caused my family leads me to think very un-Christian thoughts. It is time for me to be perfectly honest with you about how I feel.

"Eleven years ago my family was happy. Life was certainly not perfect but we all had each other and life was good. And then one day a young man named Billy walked into our lives. In this young man I saw much of myself; an adolescent quietly crying for somebody to care, to listen.

"I have to admit that the first time I met you I knew you were trouble. But I remembered my own youth, trying to gain attention through bad deeds. I tended to adopt other families in the neighborhood, trying to gain what my own family failed to provide—love and attention. That's why I never kicked you out of my house.

"Billy, you needed us. We were your substitute family. We represented a broken home with children of divorced parents that loved and worked together with discipline and respect. I think you wanted that in your own life. There were times that I had to discipline Greg because you led him into your wrong deeds, for attention's sake. There were times that I also, in an outsider's way, tried to discipline you. But I never wanted to hurt you, Billy. I only wanted to help.

"But then one day you walked into my home and killed the only things that were dear to me—my children. You cannot know the excruciating pain you caused me the night I learned I would never be with my children again. Nothing could be done to undo what you had done. When I learned that it was you who killed them, I only wanted to know why. What had we done to make you so angry? Couldn't we have talked it out and resolved it? I could think of nothing.

"The police picked you and a man named Ray up for questioning. It was now the State versus Billy and Ray. But you didn't kill the State. You killed my children! It should have been the Swifts versus Billy and Ray.

"Had it been, neither of you would have lived to be sorry. For the hurt that you caused us was so great that we would have declared you guilty on all four counts of capital murder and had you sent to the electric chair. Unless, of course, they would have allowed us to kill you personally with our bare hands. These are strong words from a Christian, but they are the way I felt at that time.

"Since that day, George and I have been put in a prison. A prison of emptiness. A prison of grief. A prison of longing to hold our children, and knowing that longing will never be fulfilled.

"But not just George and me. The children's grandparents, aunts and uncles, cousins have also been placed in that prison, each of us wanting to be released and knowing there is no parole from the broken lives we live.

"Our children are also in prison. Stephanie, Steve, Greg, Tonya, and Stacy are in the darkest prison of all. Their cells measure only three by six feet and they lie deep under the earth. They cannot run or play. They cannot laugh or cry. They cannot bring us joy. They can only sleep.

"They have no hope that maybe next month they will be paroled. Or that perhaps they may gain favor with the guard that watches over them. They cannot touch or talk to us when we go to visit them at their prison.

"We have three other children, Sandy, Matt, and Michael, who were born into their prison, never knowing what life was like before the family was sentenced to life in prison. They must live with the fact that they will never know the siblings Mom and Dad cry for. They cannot hug the older brother that we say they resemble so lovingly. They must listen as we talk to them of evil and Satan's rule, and can only hope that Satan does not reach for them, too. Only time will tell what scars they will carry into adulthood, having grown up in this prison.

"Each one of us has no hope of parole; no chance to walk away in this life. Yet we have been imprisoned innocently. None of us did anything to justify the sentences that have been handed down to us.

"You, on the other hand, are the cause of the entire incident that has imprisoned our family. You have spent the same eleven years behind locked doors serving time for what you did.

"No, Billy, I'm not ready for you to be released from prison. I doubt that I will ever really be. But it is not up to me. It's up to the State. They will not consult me in their final decision. I have no doubt that you will be released someday, against my will and George's.

"Your letters indicate you are sincerely searching for answers about forgiveness. I sincerely pray that you are. I pray every day that it is not just a con job, a scheme to harp upon the sympathies of those in the right place to secure an early release. I pray it is indeed a need to atone for what you have done.

"But I cannot judge your heart. Only God can see inside you and read your motives. I can only interpret what I see and hear. Is your heart changing? I don't know. I pray so. But I have heard too many things about you. I don't know that they are true. Perhaps only rumors. Perhaps only a tip of the iceberg. Tell me the truth about yourself, Billy. I don't want to believe a lie.

"It is up to you what you do with your life after your parole. I will have no say. My family will still be held in our prison awaiting our parole. Yes, we will be paroled someday, long after you have probably been released from your prison.

"Someday, when Jesus comes in the clouds, He will bring with Him the keys to unlock our children's three-by-six-foot cells. On that day George and I, the grandparents, aunts and uncles, cousins and siblings will finally be released from the prison that has unjustly bound us. And we will be with our precious loved ones again.

"That will be a true parole, genuine freedom from the pain you have caused. It is a parole that you too can be a part of, Billy. But it takes a changed heart. If you are truly seeking forgiveness, you should be willing to serve your time patiently, seeking not an early release from those prison walls that hold you. But rather seeking the

One who will someday come to release us all who yearn for His coming. I await in my own prison for that glorious day."

* * *

I never heard from Billy again. In late August, we received notice of Billy's parole hearing set for September 6, 1989. I couldn't afford to fly down to be there. I sent a letter, as did many relatives and friends, to protest his release. But mine was the only one that showed signs of hope.

"I have encouraged Billy to seek training and education through the system," I wrote in my letter. "To make something of himself, for I have no doubt that he will someday be released, and I have to know that he leaves that prison a changed young man.

"Billy still needs time to change. He's not yet there. He has a greater chance of changing while locked up. Billy is a schemer, has been all his life. If he does not learn to channel his scheming into a productive occupation before his release, he will be before you again someday, and still another mother will be writing to you of her fears and horrors, begging that you deny his release. I pray that God will be with you as you decide not to release Billy at this time."

The date passed without word, and I was on pins and needles waiting for the news. The outcry was not as great this time, and I feared the parole board would seize the opportunity to rid itself of the case. There would be no reversing their decision.

A tiny article in the Springfield paper indicated that Sheriff Whitten had attended the hearing to play four minutes of the taped mock interview in which Billy bragged about the killings. He was the only one who attended the hearing.

He told the parole board he had not talked to Billy for eleven years and had no way of knowing if his demeanor had changed. But the taping would give them a glimpse of the way he was in 1978 when it was made. If he had not changed, Sheriff Whitten believed Billy was a very real threat to society.

He later told us he tried to make eye contact with Billy during the hearing.

"I just wanted to see if he was still scared of 'Old Sideburns,'" Whitten said with a laugh. "But they made me sit right beside him, and I never got the chance."

A month passed before the results were made public. On October 5, the front page boldly proclaimed, "Parole Denied for Man Who

Killed Four Children." But there was more to the story than the title indicated.

"We have a policy that when we have an inmate that we declare to be dangerous, we set parole hearings every five years instead of two," said Victoria Myers, a parole board member. She said Billy's parole was denied because of "the seriousness of the offense."

* * *

On October 19, 1989, Mom wrote me a letter. Most of it was family news. But the last paragraph was about Billy.

"John Miller (our next door neighbor at the lake) goes to church with Sheriff Whitten. Whitten told him that Dyer is being monitored very closely, as they found he is getting worse and worse. He did make verbal threats against you and Dawn, and they have so much proof of his evilness that they have postponed any further parole hearings for five years and it is their intent to NEVER LET HIM GET OUT. Wonderful!"

With all the seemingly sincere letters Billy wrote, I wondered about this news. After three parole hearings, why was he suddenly found so dangerous? What could he have done to make them change their opinion of him so quickly?

I remembered Billy's offer:

"If setting a hearing off for a couple of years will help, just let me know."

Perhaps, Billy made it happen to give us another five years to heal, to give George time to let the cries of his children fade.

But if that were the case, why didn't he make his decision public to set the record straight? I couldn't know Billy's motives for sure. Only God could know because only God could judge his heart.

The battle will continue until Billy is finally paroled. Sheriff Whitten says the next hearing will be the most critical. Billy will have served over fifteen years, the standard for his sentence. There will be those who will be happy for his release, and those who will continue to cry for justice.

I will always have questions, and I will carry my fears to my grave. But I have given the gavel to God. It is up to Him to judge Billy fairly, and I trust that His decision will be the right one.

If Billy is truly sorry, like his letters say, and he makes his way into God's Kingdom, I shall rejoice with my Father for the lost sheep that was found, and welcome my brother into the Kingdom beside me. I pray with every fiber of my being that he makes it because I truly do love my brother, God's prodigal son.

On the other hand, if he is getting worse, if he hasn't turned away from his sins and turned his heart to Jesus, I must rest in the knowledge that God will eventually administer the justice that He considers fair.

Vengeance belongs to the Lord, and I feel right about that. All the anger I once carried has been taken away from me, replaced with a quiet confidence that the outcome is in God's hands.